Table of C

THE MEANING OF SERVANTHOOD 2

THE MINDSET OF A SERVANT 31

THE MASTER OF A SERVANT 59

THE MOTIVATION OF A SERVANT..86

THE MODEL OF A SERVANT 113

THE MENTALITY OF A SERVANT 140

THE MISSION OF A SERVANT..172

THE MISTAKES OF A SERVANT..197

THE MONITOR OF A SERVANT...228

HOW CAN YOU TELL A SERVANT? 231

CHAPTER 1

THE MEANING OF SERVANTHOOD

A three day global moon watch kept millions enthralled. "Apollo 15" astronauts David R. Scott and James B. Irwin were the focus of worldwide attention July 30, through August 1, 1971. Having landed on the surface of the moon in their space craft "Falcon", they proceeded to set unimaginable records. They explored 17.4 miles of the moon's surface in their little electric car. Eighteen of their 66 hours on the surface were spent outside their lunar module. Rarely had any persons been the center of so much notoriety. They were actually doing what mankind had dreamed of for centuries. As a result of their heroics and exploits, their names would forever be etched in the annals of space exploration. Virtual deification awaited them upon their return.

After piloting their space craft on its 250,000 mile journey back to planet earth, James Irwin noted, "As I was returning to earth I realized that I was a servant - not a celebrity. So I am here as God's servant on planet earth to share what I have experienced that others might know the glory of God."

Many persons, having done far less to attain celebrity status, think of themselves more highly than that. Few persons bring to clearer focus their reason for being alive than James Irwin did in this statement. Our reason for being is to serve our Creator in such a way as to enable people to come to know Him and His glory. Our role is that of a servant. The mission of a servant is to fulfill the wish of the Master.

Albert Schweitzer, a man with a servant's temperament said, "The only one among us who will be really happy are those who will have sought and found how to serve." This in part explains why there are so few truly happy persons.

Happiness is not, as the world seems to believe, something to be sought or bought, but it is a beautiful by-product of a job well done. The job to be done is that of a servant. The spin-off of a fulfilling servant lifestyle is the joy inherent in it. Finding happiness apart for fulfilling service in the name of Jesus is as impossible as finding a black palomino.

About 500 times the noun servant and the verb serve are found in the Bible. Such emphasis is put on the role of a servant because service performed in the name of Jesus rewards the worker with more real happiness and satisfaction than any other venture in life. It is the sure and safe way to the "abundant life" of which our proto-type of a servant, Jesus Christ, spoke.

Self-esteem, happiness as an end in itself, recognition, notoriety, self- assertiveness, and prosperity theology are themes that sell today. Motivated by such themes we have turned inward rather than turning loose and, as a result, we have become stagnant rather than flowing with life. Having been created to give of ourselves, we have instead become emotional statuary waiting for a proper pedestal. "How may I gain and attain" has replaced "how may I serve you in the name of my Lord."

A servant temperament more than any other trait makes for a productive person. This trait takes precedent over education, personality, and skill. It determines how effectively one will use all other admirable assets. It identifies one as having compassion, being conscientious, and showing concern. Skills can be taught but this basic characteristic must come from the core of the individual's will. A gifted person without a servant temperament cannot contribute as much to society as a less talented person with a servant temperament.

Few among those who are "making it" in our society today have servant temperaments. Musicians, athletes, politicians, and financiers with celebrity status have few numbered among their ranks who have the spirit of a servant. Exaggerated egos have become our role models. Celebrity status is often sought at the expense of conviction and character. This even trickles down into the Christian faith in subtle ways. We have failed to remember that we must forget ourselves into immortality. Only when "what can I do for you" replaces "what is in it for me" does one begin to grow as a fulfilled servant.

After Benjamin Franklin received a letter thanking him for his service he responded: "As to the kindness you mentioned, I wish I could have been of more service to you than I have been, but if I had, the only thanks that I should desire are that you would always be ready to serve any other person that may need your assistance... As for my own part, when I am employed in the service of others I do not look upon myself as conferring favors but paying debts."

When that beautiful principle is elevated to apply to our relationship with our Lord it takes on even greater meaning. What thanks our Lord desires and deserves from us as a result of His serving us so faithfully is that we should serve others in His name. Thereby He is glorified and we gratified. Nature gives us illustrations of how to live together. The principle is called commensalism. It involves living together, but neither at the expense of the other. For example there is a little salt water fish called a Gobi. The Gobi has poor eyesight and is defenseless; thus is vulnerable to predators. However, the Gobi is a superb digger. Shrimp have great eye sight and good defenses, but are poor diggers. Hence, they lack proper shelter. Commensalism results in the Gobi digging a hole in which the two live together. The Gobi provides the burrow and the shrimp serves as a look out and protector. Neither lives at the expense of the other without providing for the other.

Charlie Brown once asked Lucy, "Why are we here on earth?" A moment of contemplation was all that was necessary before Lucy answered, "Why, we are here to serve other people." Charlie Brown's forlorn look faded with his next question, "Well, then why are other people here on earth?" In part, we are here to serve one another. We are to live commensally. However, even if others don't serve us, we should not forfeit our role as servants.

The Christian community is intended to harmoniously live together serving one another -- neither at the expense of the other. However, even if there is a breakdown and some fail to serve that does not give the right to others to follow their example and retire. Christ, not they, is our model.

TRAITS OF A SERVANT

Knowing the traits of a Jewish slave enables us to better understand our function as servants of Christ. Five basic characteristics are recorded in history.

* A slave had no rights as a citizen. Our culture has a tendency to look at our rights under a magnifying glass and our responsibilities through the wrong end of a telescope.

* A slave could own no property. In truth, we are only temporary stewards of all under our control. An awareness of it being under our supervision for only a few years helps avoid selfishness.

* A slave in the eyes of the law was mere chattel which could be bought and sold as Judas did Jesus. Our real value is not determined by earth bound standards. It is in how effectively we serve our Master.

*   A slave could be scourged and tortured to death by his or her master and there was no reprisal. We too must remember we are at the mercy of the world while dependent upon the mercy of the Lord.

*   A slave was nothing less than a dead person according to the law. Only when we count ourselves as dead in Christ do we begin to live.

Slaves knew and accepted their status. They experienced little disappointment because they knew what to expect. They had no false hopes or misplaced aspirations. Their joy and fulfillment came in faithfully serving a good master. The character of the master, not the task, made the service a reward in itself. When our focus is on our Master, Jesus Christ, and not upon our role or reward, there is gratification. Our pleasure is found in pleasing Him. Life's most menial or tedious task takes on a new personality when viewed from this prospective.

TERMS FOR A SERVANT

The New Testament uses five different Greek words to speak of one who renders service. Not all of them are translated "servant," but each speaks of one providing a service. Knowing them helps to properly frame our concept of service.

DOULOS is translated bondslave or servant. Servants born in a state of slavery were called bondslaves. They were bound to their master in a relationship that could only be broken by death. This permanent bonding was ultimately made as matter of the will of the master and slave. At a certain stage of their relationship the master could offer the slave freedom, if well pleased with service rendered. At this point, the slave was free to choose whether to remain with the master of become independent. If the slave was well pleased with the master and chose to remain, a ceremony followed that marked their relationship.

The ear lobe of the slave was placed against the doorpost of the master's house and the master drilled a hole through it with an awl. The slave was thus ear- marked as the willful property of the master in a lifelong relationship.

Parenthetically, any persons wanting to use this principle as a proof text for getting their ears pierced should take the principle all the way. The hole in the ear was large enough to put a pencil through.

Once this act of commitment was complete then the slave became the property of the master, who assumed the responsible of providing for and protecting the slave. Those who are the bondslaves of Jesus Christ are likewise His property and He takes upon Himself their provisions and protection.

In a writing by George MacDonald entitled <u>Robert Falconer</u> are found these words: "This is a sane, wholesome, practical, working faith: First, it is a man's business to do the will of God; second, that God takes on Himself the special care of that man; and third, that therefore that man ought never to be afraid of anything."

Relax!

Faithful bondslaves of Jesus Christ have every right to have composure and a peace that passes understanding even amid crisis. It is when we assume responsibility for what our Master is pledged to provide that we become emotional wrecks. Commitment to His cause and confidence in His capacity consequents in composure.

The marking of a slave against a door post left blood thereon. In the Old Testament there were three occasions when blood on the door post was symbolical. The three uses indicate three characteristics of a bondslave. In Exodus 12:23 it meant I believe, in Deuteronomy 6:9 it meant I obey, and in Deuteronomy 15:17 it meant I love.

Combined, these three meant that a bondslave served the master even to the extent of disregard for his or her own interests. Rights and status had nothing to do with a servant's behavior. The issue was ownership. When that ownership was a result of a choice by the slave, service was sweeter.

Service performed by a bondslave after the ceremony of commitment was voluntary and devout, coming from a dependent and obedient servant. Our Christian experience should parallel that behavior. When such a mind-set prevails a person does not feel imposed upon or lacking in status. Fulfilled in service is the spirit of faithfulness.

When concerned with ingrates to whom we render service, we become reluctant. When preoccupied with the One in Whose name the service is rendered, there is rejoicing.

A pre-engagement mind-set enables joy in all things. Paul expressed it in Colossians 3: 23, "And whatever you do, do it heartily, as to the Lord, and not to men." That frame of reference gives stability. If we serve with enthusiasm an audience of one and that one is the Lord, emotional equilibrium results. If we do what we do as to the Lord in a manner acceptable to Him and others disapprove, we don't get depressed. We didn't do it for them, but for Him. If we do what we do in that same spirit and people approve, we don't become egotistical. We didn't do it for them, but for Him. This avoids highs and lows and gives momentum to life.

A bondslave did what was done in order to please the master and only the master. When we seek celebrity status through our lifestyle, frustration consequents. It is a clear evidence that our perspective has become clouded. When we do what we do to please our Master, we evidently have chosen our audience of One.

Always do whatever God gives you to do to the best of your ability. It is the best possible preparation for what He may have in store for you next.

DIAKONOS_is a Greek word variously translated "servant," "minister," and "deacon." The word "deacon" was first and principally used as an adjective to speak of ones activity, not an office. Later it was used as a noun referring to an office. Even then it was used to speak of one who fulfilled his office of service with such haste as to kick up dust while rushing to serve. Failure to realize the servant role of a deacon has caused much confusion in modern church life. There is no person or role more vital to the progress of a church than that of a godly deacon dedicated to serving His Lord through the church. However, when the role is misunderstood and the office considered a place of prestigious preeminence, confusion reigns. When the deacon becomes an administrative office, the church is robbed of the core of servant-leaders God intended. When thus misused, it infringes on the role of the bishop, pastor, causing further confusion. When deacons dedicate themselves to the Biblical role of pastoral- ministries rather than business administrators, the church has a functioning body of model servants.

A DIAKONOS, "servant", was one who executed the command of another. Again the issue was ownership. The slave existed to serve the master.

Jerry Clower, the former entertainer, spoke of the time he was informed that one of his children had been involved in a dramatic car wreck. As he sped to where the child was said to be, he did not know if the child was dead or alive. He said that as he drove he prayed, "Lord, help me to act like I have always told folks they should act." Fortunately the child lived. Even more fortunately, even without knowing the child would live, he acted not only like he had always told folks they should act, but like He knew His Master had told him to act. That is the way it is with a servant. Servants want to carry out the instructions of their master. They live to obey.

Many Christians have never been led to see their primary function as that of a servant of the Lord. Divided loyalties cause personal stress and community confusion. Jesus warned that "no servant can serve two masters" (Luke 16:13). As long as a believer is trying to please the world and the Lord, the Lord is never pleased.

OIKETES is the Greek word employed by Christ to assert that no person can serve two masters. It comes from the Greek root for house, OIKOS. It designated a house-servant. Such a servant held a close relationship with the family. Though the servant never forgot his or her role there was nevertheless a more personal relationship than is implied by some other titles.

In using the word, Jesus was saying you can't live in two houses at once and be loyal to both families at the same time. You have to choose. Every person serves a master. Lost sinners are described as "the servants (DOULOS) of sin" (Romans 6: 17). Sin is the master of all who have not chosen Christ to be their Master. Remember, the relationship of a DOULOS "servant" can only be broken by death. It is only when we die to self that we are freed from the slavery to sin. Until this spiritual death and new birth happens, we are captives of the power and punishment of sin.

HUPERETES is a Greek word referring to a subordinate official or slave who wanted to, and waited to, carry out the command of his superior. In the dining halls of the nobility, servants waited at the doorway to carry out the slightest wish of their master. Such servants kept their gaze fixed on their master, more specifically, the hand of the master. Hand signals were often used to give a command. For this reason the Psalmist speaks of having his eyes on the hand of the Lord. The sole purpose of existence was to serve the master, to fulfill the master's slightest wish. A devoted slave tried to anticipate the desire of the master and fulfill it before it became an evident need. There was an eagerness to do the will of the master. We need not make that application beg for understanding. We too should anticipate the desire of our Master and eagerly seek to fulfill it.

The term was also used of an orderly who attended a commander in war. The orderly lives to enable his commander to function and win his objective. He, knowing his commander's mind, tries to anticipate needs and meet them. However, when there is a command, there is no equivocation, only obedience. Believers don't have to try to anticipate certain desires of their Commander. They are simple and clear orders plainly written. When a believer comes across a Bible command, the only proper response is a snappy, "Yes, Jesus." Immediate execution is appropriate. Orderlies don't argue -- they obey.

After Santa Anna defeated the Texas force at the Alamo, he pursued the troops under the command of Sam Houston. Houston's badly outnumbered force was backed against the San Jacinto River. Cut off by the superior numbers of Santa Anna, Houston made his final battle plan. While doing so, he called his faithful orderly and close friend "Deaf" Smith and commanded him to burn the bridge behind them which crossed the San Jacinto River. Smith responded by saying that was the only way out, the only route of retreat. Houston replied, "Burn the bridge. That's not the way we are going out of here." Smith burned the bridge. Soon, thereafter, Houston gave the command that resulted in the total defeat of the Mexican army. Our beloved Lord has commanded us to burn our bridges and follow Him. As His orderlies, we have no response but "Yes, Jesus."

THERAPON is a Greek word translated "servant" in the New Testament. This title spoke of one who rendered service without regard to being slave or free. Service was performed tenderly and nobly without constraint. Moses was a THERAPON in the House of God (Hebrews 3:5). Such a title has dignity and honor to it. To be called "the servant of the Lord" was a lofty tribute. It was applied, not only to Moses, but to Job, Abraham, Isaac, and Jacob. This term for "servant" describes a position of esteem and honor. God brought Moses to the scene when His house was in disarray. As His servant, God gave Moses a great trust. He was faithful in fulfilling his office. God also trusted him to contest Pharaoh and Moses was faithful. God gave him great talent and he faithfully used it. His leadership skills, business acumen, and organizational ability were placed at the service of the Lord. Moses was also faithful in the strenuous tests given him by God. He was so devoted that he desired for his name to be blotted out of the heavenly record rather than fail to fulfill his servant role to Israel.

No higher use is made of the title than in the messianic servant-passage of Isaiah (Isaiah 42 and 52). These prophecies had their fulfillment in the person of the Son of God, Jesus Christ. In thinking of Christ as the Servant of the Lord par excellence, we must not forget He was also Son of God. His authority is that of a son though His faithfulness is that of a servant. As Son, He was sovereign by reason of His eternal relationship as co-equal with the Father. As servant, He was faithful in fulfilling His role as Mediator by being "obedient unto death, even the death of the cross" (Philippians 2: 8). His was service nobly and tenderly rendered without constraint.

Much is said in our society about "celebration." This is appropriate, but there is a much higher form of honor to be given our Lord. It is imitation. For a lost person Christ exists only as a potential Savior. Once saved He then becomes the believer's model to be imitated.

Peter said, "Christ also suffered for us, leaving us an example, that you should follow his steps" (I Peter 2:21). Charles M. Sheldon wrote a best seller in 1896 entitled In His Steps. He was motivated to write this novel by the indifference of the congregation he pastored. He properly reasoned that his beloved church membership would live more productive spiritual lives if they walked in the steps of Christ. His efforts have continued to encourage persons to follow the path plotted by Christ for them in daily conduct. The process still works.

Paul used a term in addressing the church at Thessalonica which means to imitate. He commended them for becoming "followers," that is, imitators of Christ (I Thessalonians 1: 6). This imitation does not imply merely external acting, but conduct resulting from the enabling grace of God. Without the internal enabling grace of God, any attempt to imitate Christ can only fail. Energy of the flesh emulation soon becomes exhausting. Such persons are called "apostates." An apostate is one who has known the truth and rejected it. Between the knowing and the rejecting may be a period of time during which the person gives the appearance of a believer. He might outwardly affirm Christian doctrine, but he doesn't have a heart yielded to God. An apostate has received light, but not the Life! To some degree, such a person may have received the written word, but not the Living Word.

Jesus told a parable of a sower to illustrate what an apostate is (Luke 8). One class of persons referred to in the parable is a group which "when they hear, receive the word with joy; and these have no root, who believe for a while and in time of temptation fall away." The verb form for "apostasy" is used to say they "fall away." In receiving the word they merely give intellect ascent to it. The fact that they do this with "joy" indicates they are even emotionally involved. However, they have no involvement of their will in the process. The fact they are not willfully committed to Christ is indicated by the fact they their do not bring forth fruit (Matthew 13:23). Actually, they have no roots; no life in Christ.

Such a person may even be deeply involved in church activities for a time. There are numerous Biblical examples of such persons. The entire little book of Jude deals with the subject so extensively that it might be sub-titled, "Acts of the Apostate." There are many modern examples of persons deeply involved in "selling" Christianity who have fallen away. For a period of time they gave every external evidence of being a believer. Their achievements have in some instances earned them the status of a celebrity. Their external charade inevitably is exposed and their apostate nature revealed. These are decoys of Satan and alibis of sinners. We must not be deceived by such persons for hypocrisy is the tribute vice pays to virtue. To imitate Jesus means to submit internally to Him as Lord and then seek to pattern His behavior by His enabling grace. It then becomes Christ in you Who is acting out His will through you. There is nothing synthetic or superficial about that kind of imitation.

Thomas a Kempis wrote <u>Of the Imitation of Christ</u>. His thesis is a reminder that we must copy the life of Christ. Kempis exhorts believers to "Remember that you are here to serve, not to rule; that you are called to suffer in the furnace. Here no one can abide, unless he is ready to humble himself with all his heart for the love of God."

In describing Christ's advent, John used the title for Him of "Logos" (John 1:1). To understand the meaning of a word, we are aided by observing what it meant at the time it is used. The term had little previous usage. Plato was the one who used it most definitively. He used it to speak of all that is known or knowable about God. Thus,

Jesus is all that is known or knowable about God. As such, Christ is both an example of God and an example for us to imitate.

THE TRIUMPHANT SERVANT

As our standard of servanthood, Christ evidences some basic traits His servants must have. Incorporation of these principles can be done only by willful consent to His standard.

As His service to the Father was voluntarily submissive, so must ours be. He "became obedient" (Philippians 2:8). This He did by His free choice. Mechanical means of manipulation and commercial coercion may be employed to stimulate servanthood, but only an act of the will can produce long term faithfulness.

A second trait of Christ as a servant was His total dependence. He said, "I can of Myself do nothing..." (John 5:30). If He could not of Himself, surely our fits of energy of the flesh cannot achieve the divine will. When we quit trying and start trusting Him; His empowering grace is made available. When we make known our availability, He gives us His ability. Servants don't strain, they simply submit. This does not imply passiveness or lack of involvement; it merely refers to reliance upon the Lord for His enabling grace.

A third trait of Christ as a servant was His steadfast devotion. Resolutely He said, "I must work the works of Him that sent Me" (John 9:4). A will cast in titanium is essential in order to maintain a fresh devotion. To stay when others stray evidences a will well fixed.

From the infidel pen of Friedrich Nietzsche came these words, as recorded in his work <u>Beyond Good and Evil</u>, "The essential thing 'in heaven and earth' is...that there should be long obedience in the same direction; there thereby results, and has always resulted in the long run, something which has made life worth living." A spastic, herky-jerky, on again off again fidelity dishonors the Lord, displeases the world, and defeats the doer. Consistency counts for more than capacity.

Years ago a steel beam weighing nearly a ton was suspended from a chain in a large room free of air movement. Nearby a one ounce cork was suspended on a thread. Mechanically, the cork was set in motion, swinging back and forth striking the beam each time it swung. In a matter of days, that heavy beam, in response to the consistent encounter with the cork, was freely swinging back and forth. In the realm of the spiritual, as well as, in the sphere of physics, consistency overcomes great obstacles. It was by His consistency that Christ overcame the world.

All around Christ were examples of inconsistency, but He abided faithful. Some were offended because of Him. After sharing a supernatural insight, Christ noticed His disciples murmuring and asking "Does this offend you?" (John 6:61).

Some fell away after following Him for some time (John 6:66). Then Christ uttered some of the most plaintive words of His ministry, as He addressed His disciples: "do you also want to go away? (John 6:67).

Some wavered in their walk with Christ. Once, as He walked with a group of friends along a road, He explained that the birds have their nests and the foxes their holes, but He didn't have a place to call His own where He could lay His head (Luke 9: 57 - 62. Many wavered and walked away. The rewards were not what they expected and they abandoned His cause. A servant would not have departed. Christ said, "It is enough for a disciple that he be as his teacher, and a servant like his master" (Matthew 10: 25). As He was consistently faithful, so, must His followers be if they are to be becoming of their Master.

Bill Borden, heir of the Borden Milk fortune, left his studies at Yale and spent his short life serving among the Indians as a missionary. Though a strong and successful athlete, he developed consumption and died at a young age. His last entry made in his diary the evening of his death revealed his servant temperament: "No reserve, no retreat, no regret." Such a faithful servant reveals the faithfulness of his Lord. In marveling over his abandonment of a life of luxury for servanthood, we might be struck by the words "No reserve, no retreat..." Cause for elation is found in the expression "no regret." That is the voice of a satisfied customer. He who was faithful to his Lord found His Lord to be faithful to him.

There is no service comparable to that which is the overflow of love. If we are springs, not sponges, this flow will be unfailing. Our humanity serves us falsely if it calls us to celebrity status as a sponge rather than celebrant service as a spring.

As a child, I enjoyed retreating to the back side of our farm where there was a spring which legend says was visited by the Indian Princess Osyka for whom my little home town was named. I found it a joy to sit beneath an old oak tree nearby and watch the ever-bubbling, cool water spring out of its earthly home. Its refreshing flow seemed so natural. It existed to flow in wet or dry weather. That was its reason for being and its spontaneous action. That spring is monitored in my mind as a reminder of how we must serve. The spring didn't wait to be asked to flow; it just did it because it was its nature. If we wait to perform a service we see needs to be done, we are little better off than if we had not done it at all. We live to serve.

Matthew Henry observed "If the work be done in Christ's name, the honor is due to His name." If we refuse to serve because the reward is too minimal, or the task too menial, we lack a servant's heart and dishonor our Lord. Knowing the honor is due our Lord, will not cause us to demure in doing it. Our ambition for His honor should be so strong that we will attempt any task if He gets any measure of honor. Our failure to serve that robs God of the honor of a job well done is tantamount to depriving the Lord of a portion of His glory.

Leo Tolstoy wrote the story of a Russian cobbler named Martin Avdyeeich. He lived in a cellar with a single window. From his vantage point he saw mostly boots of those who passed by. Few there were that had not been touched by his hand.

While Martin was still a journeyman his wife died. As their one son grew to be the pride of his life, he too died suddenly leaving Martin despairing and murmuring against God.

One day Martin was visited by an old peasant passing through his city. He said to Martin, "Thy speech, Martin, is not good. How shall we judge the doings of God? It is because thou wouldst have lived for thine own delight that thou dost despair." "But what is a man to live for?" inquired Martin. The old pilgrim answered, "For God, Martin. He gave thee life and for Him thou must live. Then thou wilt grieve about nothing more, and all things will come easy to thee."

The story continues with Martin finding fulfillment in serving others. He is gratified in performing the most meager service for the humblest of people for he came to realize the truth as spoken by Christ when He said, "In as much as ye have done it unto one of the least of these my brethren, ye have done it unto me." Be ye doers of the word and not hearers only.

CHAPTER 2

THE MINDSET OF A SERVANT

A night of solitude devoted to prayer ended for Jesus and the new day dawned on an assembling eager class of devotees. Or were they? They were most definitely eager hearers. Broad is the chasm between learning and doing, however. Selection was made of the twelve He would relate to most intimately. Down from the mountain they came to be greeted on the plain by a multitude seeking after healing and knowledge. From Jerusalem, Judea, Tyre, and Sidon they came. He would not disappoint them. Many were healed and all were to learn heavenly principles to apply on earth.

In the midst of that illuminating discourse, Jesus injected a question to His fledgling disciples: "Why do you call me, Lord, Lord, and do not the things which I say?" (Luke 6:46). Why, did they? More pertinently, why do we?

Why would a quarterback call a person coach and not run his play?

Why would an executive call a superior the CEO and not follow his executive order?

Why would a soldier call a ranking officer commander and not obey his command?

Why would a construction worker call someone project director and not follow his plan?

Why would a deck hand on a ship call a person captain and not follow his instructions?

Why?

Charles Spurgeon said, "Believing and obeying always run side by side." God is not first to be enjoyed, but first to be obeyed. It is obedience that brings enjoyment. Obedience, not ecstasy, is the real revelation of love. God is not to be enjoyed until He is obeyed. Love is the eye which guides the foot of obedience. Loving God and obeying God are so interwoven that each implies the other. This love produces a way of life, a life-style of obedience. Obedience is indisputable proof of uninhibited love for God.

To dramatize the challenge of obedience Jesus even referred to it as cross bearing. It must be noticed that such a warning wasn't included in the fine print on the back page. It was the bold headline of His life. The faith that works is a faith that works.

Why call Christ Master and not follow Him?

Why call Him King of Kings and not serve Him?

Why call Him Lord of Lords and not obey Him?

Why?

William Penn, founder of the state of Pennsylvania, was imprisoned in the Tower in England for his faith. There he wrote his well-known treaties of self- sacrifice entitled, "No Cross, No Crown." A later voluminous work entitled "Fruits of Solitude" contained this insight regarding servants: "A True, and a Good Servant, are the same Thing. But no servant is True to his Master that Defrauds him.

Now there are many Ways of Defrauding a Master, as of Time, Care, Pains, Respect, and Reputation, as well as Money. He that Neglects his Word, Robs his Master, since he is Fed and Paid as if he did his Best; and he that is not as Diligent in the Absence, as in the Presence of his Master, cannot be a true Servant. Nor is he a true Servant, that buys dear to share in the Profit with the Seller. Nor yet he that tells

Tales without Doers, or deals basely in his Master's Name with other People; or Connives at others Loiterings, Wastings, or dishonorable Reflections.

So that a true Servant is Diligent, Secret, and Respectful; More Tender of his Master's Honor and Interest, than of his own Profit. Such a Servant deserves well, and if Modest under his Merit, should liberally feel it at his Master's Hand."

The title Lord was used several ways in the New Testament. Use of it any way by the disciples was an acknowledgement that they owed Him their allegiance. The Greek word for Lord was KURIOS. Consider these usages. It was used as a title of respect much like our word "sir". There was honor inherent in the word. It was used of one with authority. Luke makes reference to a person who was the "lord of the vineyard". This meant he was in charge of it and had the right to exercise authority over it. A third application was to deity. Romans believed Caesar to be divine and called him Kurios Caesar. Even at this early stage of discipleship Christ's followers may have used the title in this manner. In the Greek translation of the Old Testament called the

Septuagint (LXX) the tetragrammation for Jehovah God was JHWH. The Jews held the name for God to be so sacred that they would not spell it out fully. The Greek word used to translate JHWH, the name for God, was KURIOS, Lord.

They may well have used the word to ascribe honor and glory to Jesus. Regardless of the degree of honor bestowed on Jesus by use of the title "Lord, Lord," He pressed the point of their dishonesty. Though they were confessing Him to be Lord they were not obeying Him. Legitimately, Christ pressed the question, "Why?" That question is still germane to modern day professors of faith who are not practitioners of the faith.

Our obedience honors Him.

Our disobedience disgraces Him.

Often a Christian guilty of a willful improper action will engage in self- exoneration by saying, "It is my business because it doesn't hurt anybody but me." Wrong! Big time, wrong. Industrial strength -- WRONG! Any misconduct by a person who professes to follow Christ becomes the business of Christ and the church. Behavior unbecoming of our Lord becomes Satan's insulation between the lost world and Christ. It is the alibi of the unregenerate.

Those who pretend to honor Christ by calling Him Lord dishonor Him by not obeying Him. His cause would be better off if such a one had never named His name only to defame His name. Public repentance is essential for recovery by a genuine believer who has faltered and failed in an instance. The sphere of that confession should be as big as the region of its knowledge. Often that involves righting the matter with only one person while at other times it might involve confession before the entire church. Such an act would be humbling to the repentant Christian, but even that is honoring to the Lord. Foremost in our thoughts must be His honor. God thinks most of the person who thinks of self as least.

The sun wasn't the only thing hot on the plain that day. Christ's searing question burned itself into their consciences. Doubtless it was later recalled as they set out on their post-resurrection ministry. It served as a standard of excellence. The perpetual challenge was to make profession and practice one and the same. The more exactly profession and practice are aligned the more obvious is obedience to Him as Lord.

On a wet roadway a well aligned car will show only one set of treads on each side. This indicates the back tire in properly aligned with the front and is following exactly in line with it. That is the way profession and practice must be aligned.

Illustrations of servants abounded in the disciples' world. Regularly they saw persons of authority attended by servants. It was not uncommon for teachers to emerge who gained a following of loyal supporting disciples. John the Baptist, the forerunner of Christ, had disciples as did others before him. Jesus, and Jesus alone, deserves such loyalty. Periodically a new guru from the Orient emerges in America to which unlimited obedience is shown. Possessions are sold and given these false prophets, families forsaken, and positions abandoned in order to align with these mystical gurus. Our beloved Lord Jesus alone deserves such obedience. He will never misguide a loyalist as did these misguided guides. Tragedy of tragedies is that most persons who follow the pretentious prophets are looking for the love and acceptance intended to be given by the church in Christ's name. I have never talked with a member of a cult that did not have the same reason for joining. They never say it was their pure doctrine or the great principals advocated. It is always "they accepted me and made me feel like somebody." Church members, in the name of Christ, must show such compassionate acceptance of outsiders. Their conduct may be repugnant to any believer and abhorrent to the Lord but they, the person, must be loved. Why do we call Jesus Lord and not love the least, the last, and the lost?

A massive segment of society is mirrored in the pathos of an unlikely song from the animated "Mr. Mago's Christmas Carol":

"A hand for a hand was planned for the world,

Why don't my fingers reach?

Millions of grains of sand in the world, Why such a lonely beach?

Where are two shoes to click to my clack?

Where is a voice to answer mine back?

I'm all alone in the world."

We could embrace and stroke Mr. Mago in this plaintive mood, but how   about the less cuddly with the same need?

Kings, presidents, and over fifty members of Congress worship in ourfellowship. No one of them should be made to feel more loved than the humblest person of the most meager rank who enters the building. Christ said, "Inasmuch as you d i d n o t d o i t one of the least of these, you did not do it to Me (Matthew 25:45).

Old Testament truths formed a background against which Christ's disciples could assess their relationship with Him. Psalm 123 was commonly known in their time. When it becomes as well known in our time as Psalm 23 we might add practice to our praise of the Lord. Three traits of a servant are self-evident in the Psalm.

A SERVANT IS DEVOTED

With aspiration and admiringly the psalmist says, "Unto thee lift I up my eyes..." (Psalm 123:1).

An upward look implies adoration, an inward trust, faith and confidence. Servants knew their masters were superior. That issue was never in question. The issue was ownership. Obedience was part of that package.

Household servants were reared with a certain mentality. They were trained how to serve, but also they served because they had an instinct to do it. It was their nature. They did not do so simply to obey; they did it because they had a servant's temperament and mentality. Knowing it to be their role, they did it naturally. Service from such a nature was reflexive and spontaneous. They thought nothing of it. It was their reason for living.

In ancient Egypt servants of a Pharaoh were buried alive with their deceased ruler. This invokes protest and resistance in our thought. Not having their mentality, it is an abhorrent idea to us. To them it was a joyous and willing part of serving such a one. They had the mentality of a servant.

When we realize that we must die not at the end of our days but today, then we begin to live. At that point, we take our stance in the shadow of the cross; our whole life becomes an advent; and we live looking forward to our Easter which issues in eternal life.

A captive slave brought into service against his or her will struggled against authority. Force, even brutality had to be used to drive them to service. Rewards were few and reprisals many for coerced service.

When we come to Christ we come out of a self-willed world where we have been looking out for number one. Egotism, self-centeredness, and false personal pride, typify the world mentality. While climbing the ladder of success, we will lick the boots of those on the rung above us and stomp the hand of the one beneath us. Worldly success has a glare about it that dazzles the eyes of persons oriented to it. Success at any price and at the expense of anybody goes in worldly arenas. To ascend is no sin no matter how you do it. That is the world's way.

Living in that environment and being converted from that culture, we come to Christ bringing that mentality. It struggles with the attitude of being a servant. A celebrity mentality and a servant temperament can't co-exist. Upon coming to Christ, we cease looking inward and start looking upward. For some this is instantaneous. For others it is a struggle. For the pretenders it never works for long. It can't be managed by the energy of the flesh; it must be motivated by love which prompts obedience. One in love with Christ doesn't feel constrained to conform externally, but is internally compelled by love to comply.

There was a cartoon in "New Yorker Magazine" with the caption "Nannook Goes South". It was one of those multi-frame cartoons. In the first, Nannook was pictured in his native cold north country wearing a heavy parka. A subsequent frame showed him in the sunny warm south wearing that same warm parka. The caption notes he is "boiling in his parka, but old habits die hard". A bit of Nannook lives in all of us. Only Christ can enable us to overcome this "Nannook complex".

Jack Paar, former TV talk show host, said, "Looking back, my life seems like one long obstacle course, with me as the chief obstacle." When it comes to servanthood there is no greater hindrance than self.

Part of servanthood consists in learning how the master wants things done, how he does them, and doing them his way. That is called discipleship. Basically to become a disciple is to become a duplicate.

It is more than learning what the teacher knows, or even doing what he does. It is becoming what he is. As our Lord, Jesus is the One like Whom we must aspire to become. In order to do so we must observe Him, listen to Him, and obey Him. To become what He is, His word must be our will. Servanthood without scholarship is a tree without root. Scholarship without servanthood is a tree without fruit.

For a servant/disciple the Bible becomes the procedures manual. If we accept what we like in the Bible and reject what we dislike, it is not the Bible we believe but ourselves. If we do only those things commanded by Christ which we like and disobey those we dislike, it is not Christ we are obeying but our own self-will. An authentic disciple is not a seeker after abstract truth, but after truth as a life force.

A true servant/disciple looks up to his master. You may have been looking back in disappointment. You may have been looking forward in despair. You may have been looking within in despondency. These habits can only be broken by looking up in delight.

A SERVANT IS DEPENDENT

The inspired psalmist also said "the eyes of servants look to the hand of their masters" (Psalm 123: 2). This figure of speech is like saying, "I am looking to you for help". It is a reference to being dependent upon the master for all the necessities of life. A servant had no resource or recourse other than his master. For this reason a servant looked to his master for provisions.

The servant/psalmist asked for God's mercy three times in this brief psalm. He was looking up to a God he knew comes down to get involved with His people. It is evident in the text that the psalmist was a victim of severe slander and ridicule. Plaintively the penman cries out, "We are exceedingly filled with contempt. Our soul is exceedingly filled with the scorn of those that are at ease, with the contempt of the proud" (Verses 3,4).

All of us have felt like the author of this expressed agony. Perhaps our need was not related to the same need, but it was just as real. Our reliance must be just as steadfast. A person with such faith soon comes to realize the truth of Romans 8: 18: "For I consider that the sufferings of this present time are not worthy to be compared with the glory which shall be revealed in us." The more we depend upon the Lord the more dependable we find Him to be. The more dependable we realize Him to be the more we depend upon Him. The breakdown is at the startup point. We want Him to prove His dependability before we will depend on Him. That is like a person in a cold mountain shack saying to a wood stove "You give me heat and I will give you fuel." We must first give the Lord the fuel of our dependence and then He gives the heat of His dependability. As used in this regard, dependence is a synonym for confidence, trust, and faith. Our dependence upon Him is in itself an act of obedience.

Consider your cares. Do you handle them as commanded: "Casting all your care upon Him; for He cares for you" (I Peter 5:7). Is that what you do? Are you dependent upon Him to care for your cares? To trust Him is to evidence obedient dependence.

Do you depend upon Him for guidance as instructed: "Trust in the Lord with all your heart, and lean not on your own understanding.

In all your ways acknowledge Him, and He shall direct your paths" (Proverbs 3: 5,6). God will order your steps and stops if you set your course by His star and not the lights of the city. Don't dare try to chart your course without the Bible as your sextant, your GPS, and Christ as your polar star.

In matters requiring patience do you respond as urged: "Wait on the Lord: be of good courage, and He shall strengthen your heart: wait, I say, on the Lord" (Psalm 27: 14). Sometimes waiting on the Lord isn't optional. Our attitude is always optional. To be of good courage evidences obedient dependence. It is a witness of our confidence in our Lord.

In matters of uncertainty and time of apprehension do you react as instructed: "Fear not; for I am with you; be not dismayed; for I am your God: I will strengthen you, yes, I will help you, I will uphold you with My righteous right hand" (Isaiah 41:10). An achieving life is not one that goes forward with immunity from fear. It is one which overcomes fear by faithful obedience and reliance upon the Lord for strength for the journey. God has said He will "strengthen...help...uphold". Depend upon it.

Anybody can brag of his confidence in his doctor. It is only when life is yielded to his prescribed treatment that dependence is shown. Anyone can boast of his confidence in his lawyer. It is only when he complies with his instruction that dependence is shown. Anyone can bluster of his confidence in his Lord. It is only when he does the things He says that dependence is shown. The caption of the dependent life is, YES, LORD.

Jesus said, "Most assuredly, I say unto you, The Son can do nothing of himself..." (John 5: 19). He realized His dependency upon the Father in His earthly state. Who are we to talk about doing without Him when we are dependent upon Him for the next breath we take. No person can be and do what God wants him to do until becoming dependent upon the Lord for the doing. You never will see Jesus at His best until you depend upon Him in the worst of conditions.

Every believer can say: "Jesus Christ is the Captain of my salvation, and to the cadence of His drum I will dependently march.

By the pointing of His guiding finger, I will be dependently directed. He, being my helper, I want to tread dependently in his footsteps. Lead on, O, King Eternal."

Jesus called a rich man a fool because he failed to acknowledge his dependence on God. The unwise farmer acted as though he had devised the seasons, made fertile the soil, commanded the rain, set the earth spinning on its axis to time the rising and setting of the sun, and spoke into reality the life principle of the seed. Such arrogant independence is an intellectual dead-end street. America's market place, nevertheless, currently depicts this mentality. We must be certain that the church does not reflect it. Personally we must guard against such spiritual superciliousness.

By stressing our dependence upon the Lord, it may appear that mankind is being degraded. That is not the case. The fact of man's dependence upon God is counterbalanced by God's faithfulness to man. That means they relate to each other. The fact that man, the dependant creature, can relate to God, the dependable Creator, elevates mankind. It means we are the loftiest of all created beings. The more glory and honor we appropriately ascribe to God the more noble our role.

"Every good gift and every perfect gift is from above, and comes down from the Father of lights, with whom is no variation, or shadow of turning" (James 1: 17). In light of that text make a brief inventory of good things in your life. God is their source. Appropriate praise belongs to Him. He has given them to you perhaps without your even being aware that you were dependent upon Him for them. Our capacity to "assume" is a major hindrance to a spirit of gratitude.

Jesus taught that the greater our dependence and the more consistent our dependability the surer would be His supply. For that reason He urged that we seek "first the kingdom of God, and his righteousness, and all these things shall be added unto you" (Luke 18:30). If we don't subtract from His Lordship He will add to our servanthood great joy.

To help us more fully understand our dependence upon Him, Christ likened our relationship with Him to that of a branch to a vine: "I am the vine, you are the branches. He that abides in Me, and I in him, b e a r s much fruit; for without Me you can do nothing" (John 15: 5).

Fruit bearing is not only possible for a branch that abides in a vine, it is the inevitable. When the Christ-life permeates a servant, spiritual productivity is certain; service is reflexively natural. A natural progression is root, shoot, and fruit. No more complete image of total dependence can be found than that of the branch upon the vine. A vine gives life to the branch and then enables it to bear fruit. There never comes a time when the branch is independent of the vine. Without this vital union the branch is nothing of itself. Together they form one living and life giving organic union. The fact that the vine bears fruit through the branch means the Lord entrusts His servant to bear spiritual fruit in His name. Christ is the empowering source enabling the fruit. Our interrelated union with Christ is graphically depicted in this description.

When ego takes over and there is a mental rush wish for celebrity status, remember what a branch is without the vine. Not only is it unproductive, it is lifeless. At first the branch may not know it, but soon like a cut flower it will show it.

A SERVANT IS DESIROUS

A third expression is used by the servant oriented psalmist as he says "the eyes of a maiden are upon the hand of her mistress; so our eyes wait upon the Lord our God" (Verse 2).

Rather than using verbal command oriental mistresses often gave their servants hand signals. In his letters on Egypt, Savary, an ancient traveler to that land wrote: "The slaves, having their hands crossed on their chest, stand silently at the end of the hall. With their eyes fastened on their Master, they seek to anticipate his every wish."

Servanthood was their life. Their life was for service. They did not wait to get off duty. Their lives were their duty -- their duties their lives. They lived to serve.

We must learn to let our Lord deal with us as we appear in our prayer life to want to deal with Him. We spend much of our prayer time saying in effect, "Lord, here is what I want you to do." If God has the sense of humor I imagine Him to have, He must sometimes want to say, "Wait just a minute, which one of us is God." Our prayer life should consist of "Lord, what would you have me do?" God is not a super cop to rescue us when danger threatens. He is our Lord. He is not a rabbit's foot to be taken out and rubbed when we need good luck. He is our Lord. He is not a humorist to entertain us in our melancholy moments. He is our Lord. He is not a parachute to be relied upon when all else fails. He is our Lord. No indication of resenting or resisting our Lord should be noticeable. Instead, like the Egyptian slaves we should seek to anticipate His will and execute accordingly. When a command is explicit, our reaction should be instantaneous. His command should be considered an opportunity to do something worthwhile.

A Christian with a servant temperament is the freest person in all the world. He is free to do what he wants and that is to serve his Lord. What his Lord wants him to do is always, without exception, the best thing for him to do. Our Lord in His Word never one time asks us to do one thing that is not for our good. What is for our good is for His glory also. Likewise, what is for His glory is for our good. When a person gets to the place he really wants to do what the Lord wants done, that is a joyous stage. Those not there yet can get there by doing what they know to be right. This starts the cycle. By doing the right, joy results. Joy consequents in a desire to please. A desire to please results in willful service.

This indicates our need isn't for more freedom, but for more love for the Lord we profess to serve. Being free to serve voluntarily is great freedom. No person gives self to service without first having tasted Christ's love. It creates an appetite for service.

Having dealt with theory, we now turn to practice. Consider the following areas of service and how you can relate to each in a practical way. Are you willing to obey Him in:

THOUGHTS. Paul exhorts us to engage in "Casting down arguments, and every high thing that exalts itself against the knowledge of God, bring every thought to the obedience of Christ" (II Corinthians 10: 5). It is time to move out of the mental mythological world of vain imagination and face reality. Fantasizing must be forsaken and all improper thoughts brought under the control of Christ. We are urged to have the mind of Christ in us (Colossians 2:5). That does not mean we think about Christ at all times, but it does mean we endeavor to think like Christ about everything we do. An athlete in the heat of a close contest doesn't have time to think about Christ -- he must concentrate on his assignment. If he has the mind of Christ, that determines how and what he thinks of his assignment.

It is in the closet of our minds that the first step of obedience or disobedience is taken. If we bring every thought unto captivity of Christ, the resultant step will be one of obedience. Thus, what one thinks about money becomes the Christ thought. What one thinks about sex becomes a thought under captivity to Christ. What one thinks about a person is guided by submitting the opinion to Christ for approval.

Don't let your mind dwell on anything which, if it became your action, would disgrace your Lord. By dwelling on it, the likelihood of its becoming conduct is increased. If the thought is brought under the control of Christ, the potential conduct will remain under His control.

TRUTHS. Peter commended his colleagues and challenged them and us by saying, "Since you have purified your souls in obeying the truth through the Spirit in sincere love of the brethren, love one another fervently with a pure heart" (I Peter 1: 22). By obeying the truth, they had outgrown pretense. Their love was "sincere," that is real and not play acting; it was genuine. Their love was purged by obeying the truth.

In an era when Christianity has several "camps" it is essential that regardless of where a brother pitches his tent he must be loved. We must be mature enough to discern between loving a person and not liking some of the things that person does or even believes. I find it not only necessary to love those who oppose us, but to accept their love. To say "I love you" does not mean "I agree with you on everything." Increasingly, persons repudiate gestures of love, if offered by those who do not align themselves with them.

For generations European theologians have been ahead of our Western behavior. They can fervently debate and energetically oppose one another regarding an issue and get up and go get a cup of tea together. The idea of "I won't like you unless you are like me" is contrary to Christ's command.

Peter commends them for their brotherly love (PHILEO) and charges them to have divine love (AGAPAO). They had mastered the practice of loving one another with brotherly love (PHILEO), but the further command was "that you love (AGAPAO) one another with a pure heart fervently." This is indication that we must love even if our brotherly love is rejected, for AGAPE love gives simply because it is its nature to do so, not in order to get. It also indicates we must be willing to accept the love of a brother who disagrees with us - one who pitches his tent in the land of Goshen.

TRIALS. Christ instructed us that a servant should be like his master. The unknown author of Hebrews states an example of our Master which we are to follow: Though He was a Son, yet He learned obedience by the things which he suffered" (Hebrews 5:8).

We do well to remember the old bromide "God had only one Son and not even He was immuned from suffering" the next time we suffer. Suffering legitimately prompts questions. That is natural. The problem is that we ask the wrong question. We cry out, "Why?" That is the question of science. In answering Job when he posed that question God said in effect, "I don't owe you an answer to that." The question we must train ourselves to ask is, "How? Now that this has happened, how can it be used of you Lord to help conform me to your beloved image." How is a question of theology. Suffering is a school room in which some of the most difficult, but profitable lessons are learned. No person audits this course. Those assigned it have been shown great trust by their Lord who wants to teach them therein. Not only does He want to teach them, He also wants to teach those who are class observers. Our obedience to Him under adversity often reveals His adequacy like nothing else. When we, like Christ, accept suffering and let Him carry us through it rather than resisting or refusing it, then it is transformed. By learning obedience through it, we show we have accepted it as our teacher. Only then it ceases to be suffering and becomes part of our growing self. Though it may have been intended for evil God can use it for our good.

The challenge and condemnation the disciples heard on the plain that day eventually became their call to arms. When He instructs and directs the only answer from a servant is "Yes, Lord". Anything else is treason. "No, Lord" is a contradiction in terms. If our response is "no" we are not allowing Him His role as Lord in our life. If our answer is "Lord" obedience is natural. "Lord" means "You are the God Whose authority I respect and respecting it I obey it". To say no is for the branch to say to the vine "I will not bear your fruit". Any healthy branch in union with the vine can't help but bear its fruit.

Keep your eyes on the hands of your Lord. His command is always in your best interest. Set your mind on His will and He will guide you as His devoted, dependent, and desirous servant.

CHAPTER 3

THE MASTER OF A SERVANT

It was an absorbing moment when Christ addressed the cosmopolitan crowd on the slope overlooking the scenic Sea of Galilee. Northward could be seen snowcapped Mt. Hermon lifting its head into the heavens. Behind Him was the sparkling azure blue water of Galilee. Southward the Jordan River flowed skirting the verdant valley of Esdraelon in which the final battle of Armageddon will be fought. Now, however, He speaks to them about an individual battle which must perpetually be fought. It is a mental battle to choose a master. A major grid on which His message is structured must have gripped the imagination of His listeners.

He spoke of a choice involving emotions: "...where your treasure is, there will your heart be also" (Matthew 6:21). An option is available regarding emotional involvement.

A second rapier-like thrust followed regarding an intellectual choice: "The light of the body is the eye. If therefore your eye is good, your whole body w i l l be full of light" (Matthew 6:22). The eye was analogous to the mind. An appeal is made for single mindedness.

In short order comes a third thrust related to a choice of the will: "No man can serve two masters: for either he will hate the one, and love the other; or else he will be loyal to the one, and despise the other. You cannot serve God and mammon" (Matthew 6: 24). This third dividing line called for a definitive determination regarding devotion. NO person can serve two masters, but every person must serve one. Attachment to one means detachment from the other. Single ownership makes dual service unreasonable. Duals service makes single ownership unreal.

Selection of a master must be and is made by every person. Serving a master isn't optional. It is simply a matter of choice as to which one will be served. This decision is to be made by our choice, not His coercion.

In stating this principle, Jesus also identified the only two options: "God and mammon". God is a summary for the Godhead: the Father, Son, and Holy Ghost. Mammon is also used as a summary term. It comes from the Greek word "mamona", a derivative from the Chaldean word for "the money-god". It is a synonym for materialism or things of the world order. Actually, it speaks of any and all things as opposed to the Lord. One of these two is the god of every person.

Rebellious skeptics might profess to be their "own person". That "person" then is their god. By asserting their freedom, they are declaring their commitment to a god other than the Lord. Those who have "self" as their god are invariably let down.

The only way to be free is to be bound. Over the entrance to the courthouse of Cuyahoga County in Cleveland, Ohio, are engraved these words: "Obedience To Law Is Liberty". A local judge pointed out that this was a misquote from Richard Hooker. The original statement included one other word: "Obedience To Divine Law Is Liberty." In Christ you are set free to be all that He intended you to be. This makes for a rich, full, and more meaningful life. Once Christ is chosen as your Master, He then goes to work to enable you to live what He called "the abundant life".

At that juncture, one can understand and experience what Hudson Taylor meant when he said, "It is not what Hudson Taylor does for God that matters, but what God does through Hudson Taylor." If you would serve, you must surrender. If you would overcome, you must obey. Once He is chosen as Master and allowed control over your life you don't experience overwork, but overflow.

Mammon is a cruel master. It is selfishly enslaving. Christ makes a creative Master. He is supernaturally enabling.

"Pistol" Pete Maravich was a three time all-American at LSU in basketball, player of the year, NCAA career leading scorer, who played ten years in the NBA. After retiring from the NBA, he was inducted into the Hall of Fame. He was perhaps further ahead of his game than any athlete ever in any sport. This pilgrimage lead him to a saving faith in Christ. The night after I baptized him, we sat in my study until after midnight with his asking one question after the other about Scripture. Suddenly, this man, whose career I and millions had admired, reflexively stood up and forcefully struck his fist against the palm of his other hand exclaiming, "Man, was I great!" (No one can successfully argue with that). He continued, "Man, was I great! But just think how good I could have been if my life had been right with the Lord then." Pete was acknowledging that Christ makes us better at whatever we are doing if we allow Him to be our Master. He brings out the best in a person. Only when we willfully bring our life under His mastery can our own life be mastered. Until that moment, with mammon as master, we are a walking uncivil war. Even with Christ as your Master you may never be the best at anything, but you can be your best at everything. Conversely, with mammon as master, frustration, anxiety, and anger characterize the servant's life.

ADMIT

Admit which master you serve.

By default you may be serving mammon. If you are not serving Christ, "mammon" in whatever form manifested is your master. Service to master mammon is anarchy. It is life without rules, but with confusion. Bob was riding with his friend Bill one day. Bill sped through a red light. Bob gasped, "You just ran a red light!" Bill replied, "Yeah, I know, me and my brother always run red lights." A moment later it happened again and Bob protested once more. Bill responded, "I told you me and my brother always run red lights." Just then they approached a traffic light as it turned green and Bill came to a screeching halt. "Why," asked Bob, "if you run red lights do you stop for green lights?" With a wry smile Bill replied, "Because you can't even tell when my brother may be coming down the side street."

That bit of wit depicts the chaotic "free" world of those persons blinded and bound by mammon.

Satan dupes some who serve mammon into thinking they have no god. Even a professed atheist has a god as well as a religion. His religion is atheism. Most atheists are absorbed in it. They work at convincing themselves and others there is no God. It is incumbent upon them to do so, or they would have to admit their guilt before a holy God. Many of them are enjoying the temporary pleasures of serving their god too much to want to admit their guilt and turn to a new Master. They are thus bound by the habituating chains of carnality. Kept in captivity for inevitable destruction, they must do all possible to deny a loving God who wants to set them free in time and for eternity.

Admit it, if mammon is your god. Are you satisfied with your present life and pleased with your future plight?

As there are only two optional gods, so, there are only two optional retirement plans: heaven or hell. Not even the devil will enjoy hell. It is revealed that at the end of the ages the Lord will bind Satan "And cast him into the bottomless pit, and shut him up, and set a seal on him...And the devil, who deceived them, was cast into the lake of fire and brimstone...and shall be tormented day and night forever and ever" (Revelation 20: 3 & 10). Not even he will enjoy the ultimate anarchy of hell. Admit that Jesus Christ would be a more loving Master.

In time He served as a role model of a servant in that He took upon Himself the form of a servant and became obedient (Philippians 2: 7, 8). He became what we are to be in order that we might come to be where He is.

When I left for college to play basketball, I talked with my cousin Walter who had played on the same college team as my soon-to-be new coach. Walter said, "Don't ever hesitate to do what Luke asks you to do. He has done it much more than he will ever ask you to do." Likewise, Jesus never asks us to do anything He hasn't done -- and better. Don't be squeamish about service. Don't be selfish with your time. Don't be small with your thoughtfulness. Do try giving yourself away -- in Jesus name. Who is your master? There is a definitive way to tell. It doesn't matter who you say your master is. What you do reveals who it is. Everything else is just religious talk. Here is the test to determine your master.

"Do you not know, that to whom you present yourselves slaves to obey, you are that one's slave to obey, whether of sin to death, or of obedience to righteousness" (Romans 6: 16). Identity of one's god is made by service. Many who profess Christ to be their Master are in reality serving mammon. Others engage in conflicting fits of service. They bear a more confusing witness than one who outright serves mammon. What Christ seeks is consistency. What the world craves is an uncompromising commitment to Christ as an example by which to steer. We say they should not look at us and they should not. However, in reality they have every right to, and they do. Expect it, rejoice over it, and by your life- style discredit critics of your faith.

The one you obey is your master. Who you obey reveals where your heart is and how your mind is fixed. Faithful service is needed in a "show-and-tell" culture. If Christ is your Master, serve Him. Service in His name is actually rendered unto "the least of these."The scope of the field of service was defined by Edna St. Vincent Millay who wrote: "The world stands out on either side no wider than the heart is wide".

Love for the Master is the only thing with sufficient motivating force to propel us into a field of service. On the wall of an administrative office at Southern Tech in Marietta, Georgia, hangs this quote by Pierre Teilhard De Chardin: "Someday, after we have mastered the winds, the waves, the tides, and gravity, we will harness for God the energies of love and then for the second time in the history of the world, man will have discovered fire."

Revealed wisdom is evidenced by that hanging in the office on the campus of the institution which graduates more engineering students than any university in the world. Right in the heart of what is mechanical is a statement of that which makes it all meaningful.

A practical application of this love occurred some years ago when a Salvation Army worker found a young woman lying helplessly abandoned on a city street. She leaned over and whispered to the sobbing discard, "Jesus loves you." She then gently kissed her on the brow and upon seeing slow response helped her to her feet. A bond began which resulted in that human reject receiving Christ as Savior. Later she told the Salvation Army worker, "I didn't care when you told me that God loved me. It wasn't until you showed me He did that it mattered". There is a big bruised, bewildered, and bleeding world awaiting your demonstration.

Paul's exhortation to the Romans needs to be finished: "But God be thanked, that though you were the slaves of sin, yet you obeyed from the heart that form of doctrine which you were delivered. And having been set free from sin, you became the slaves of righteousness. I speak in human terms because of the weakness of your flesh. For just as you have presented your members slaves of uncleanness, and lawlessness leading to more lawlessness, so now present your members slaves of righteousness for holiness. For when you were the slaves of sin, you were free in regard to righteousness. What fruit did you have then in the things of which you are now ashamed? For the end of those things is death" (Romans 6: 17 - 21).

These were people who "were slaves to sin" and thus "free from righteousness". Such persons being preoccupied with their freedom from obedience to Christ become so lethargic that they are unaware of being "slaves to sin".

Rejoice! This not only is what they "were", it is the state of slavery from which any person willing can be delivered. They "were delivered" because they "obeyed from the heart that form of doctrine which was delivered" to them. They heard the word of the Master and decided to "yield" themselves to Him as His "servants".

Christ, the Master, has heavenly retirement benefits. Some people think Heaven might be boring. Not so! It is well prepared. "Eye has not seen, nor ear heard, nor have entered into the heart of man, the things which God hath prepared for those who love him" (I Corinthians 2: 9)." He has it all "prepared" and waiting for those who serve Him.

Skeptics, upon thinking there will be no Super Bowls; no tractor pulls; no Final Four; no iPones; no posture-pedic clouds; no white tunics and no smell of bacon frying, find little appealing about Heaven. They think it might be boring. That is because of a limited perspective.

Try describing a sumptuous smorgasbord to a recluse from the upper Amazon who subsists mainly on berries and monkey meat. His response might well be, "Sounds boring. No monkey meat and berries".

The term "heaven" occurs over four hundred times in the four gospels. Most often it comes from the lips of Jesus. Upon His exodus from planet earth He said, "I go to prepare a place for you" (John 14: 3).

Not only has He prepared a place for His people, He is preparing His people for the place. Much legitimate mystery exists about heaven and our state there. John in love has pulled back the curtain just enough to let us have a satisfying insight. He wrote, "...it has not yet been revealed what we shall be: but we know that, when He is revealed, we shall be like Him" (I John 3: 2). Those who awake in His likeness will be satisfied.

COMMIT

In Romans 6, transferral of masters and associated servant transformation is transacted the moment one is willing to "yield". It is a time of choosing a new authority, a new base of loyalty, a new center of allegiance -- Jesus Christ. Such a decision must be:

THOUGHT OUT. This being life's biggest decision it should not be approached casually. Every line of logic points to Christ as the superior Master. Three forces seek to restrain persons and keep them from this proper choice. They are the world, the flesh, and the devil. These allies of mammon are formidable.

BROUGHT OUT. Some persons are reluctant to go public with a commitment to Christ. Certain personality types are shy and retiring. However, the grace of God can overcome this. Occasionally, there are those who demure in making an open declaration of their devotion to Christ saying it is a personal decision. It must be conceded that this is life's most personal decision. However, in the New Testament this personal decision was never a private one. Strength is gained by making an open break with the past and commitment to the new. This challenges the person making a break by giving him something to live up to.

WROUGHT OUT. Once the decision is made then we should expend every effort and exert all influence possible for our new liberating Master. When the mind-set to serve Christ is formed, joy comes from expression of love for Him manifested in service.

WELL-FOUGHT OUT. Follow through with commitment. Sign up once and for all for a life time of service freely rendered. This is done with an awareness it does not save. It is an act of gratitude for being saved. To assume our good works can save us makes God and us look bad. It makes God look bad in that it appears He can be bought off. It makes us look bad by appearing that everything we do is done to gain some favor. Grace salvation makes God and us look good. Therefore, we don't work in an effort to be saved, but out of gratitude for having been saved by grace.

SUBMIT

Dr. Elton Trueblood defined for us three elements involved in a choice to serve Christ: "No vital Christianity is possible unless at least three aspects of it are developed. These are the inner life of devotion, the outer life of service, and the intellectual life of rationality".

An inner life of devotion must be maintained. The term "maintained" is used in the same way a car must be maintained. It has to be worked on.

Prayer is one means. Prayer is not so much simple submitting our list of needs to God as it is submitting ourselves. It is more than asking God to run errands for us. It is a time of acknowledging our willingness to run errands for Him. The storehouse of God is open to His servants who pray.

Praise is a means of maintaining the inner life of devotion. We should not wave the palm branches of praise unless we are willing to wear the robes of a servant daily. Praise saves us from self-absorption. Praise evidences we have our priorities in the right order.

Worship is yet another means of maintaining the inner life of devotion. Often a church bulletin will bear the heading "11:00 AM Service." Worship is a service. Service is worship. Though all of life is worship offered the Creator by His grateful creation there needs to be a formal time of worship: a time to encounter Him in assembly with other servants. A mind preoccupied with worship of the All Mighty can't be fixed on mammon. Public worship enables us to walk through the world as though it is God's temple and therein all of life is an act of worship.

Witnessing is an essential means of maintaining the inner life of devotion. Sharing who and what Christ is to you is witnessing. Christ does not call us to isolation when He appeals to us to come out of the world. He is appealing to us to avoid fraternization. We are to penetrate the world without becoming part of it. We must live what we attempt to give. The real mark of a servant is to live in such a way as to make others want to become servants of your Master.

An outer life of service flows from an inner life of devotion. Many of the things summarily spoken of by the term "mammon" make good instruments in the hands of devoted servants. They make a poor master, but they are blessings if mastered by Christ's servant for His use. Having saved us, He leaves us here to manage His possessions. Everything we have should be looked upon with the attitude: "Master, what do you want me to do with this possession of yours?" When that with which you have been entrusted becomes that in which you trust, it has become your god.

A missionary was witnessing to a native chief in a primitive culture. The chief offered gifts of blankets, jewelry, and horses. The missionary wisely said, "My God does not want the chief's blankets, jewelry, and horses. My God wants the chief himself". Instinctive wisdom guided the chief's response, "You have a very wise God, for when I give Him myself, He also gets my blankets, jewelry, and horses". God wants the assets He has put in our trust not in order to take them away from us but to enable us to use them for their highest good. When they are yielded to Him, they are glorifying to Him and gratifying to us.

Counsel originally given young Timothy deserves our acceptance. "Let as many servants as are under the yoke count their masters worthy of all honor, that the name of God and his doctrine be not blasphemed" (I Timothy 6:1). Though this advice was given originally to servants of men it has a higher application of our Master.

Lovingly, Christ looked into the inquisitive eyes of a rich young ruler who inquired about following Him. To Christ it was evident "mammon" was the god of the admirable young man. (Mark 10: 17 - 22). Christ challenged him to change masters by divesting himself of his old money-god. The shadow of a great disappointment darkened his brow and his youthful enthusiasm faded. He let chloroforming conformity, as subtle and deadly as gasses used in chemical warfare, kill his response regarding a life of service. He knew what he needed, but he would not let go of what he wanted. This fracture in his faith led to futility.

An outer life of service opens the inner chamber of fellowship to those who choose to serve Christ. Franklin D. Roosevelt had a constant companion named Harry Hopkins. Gruffly,

Windle Wilkey asked the president, "Why do you keep that frail sickly Harry Hopkins at your elbow?" Instantly, the chief executive gestured toward the door and replied, "Hundreds come through that door daily who want something from me. Harry Hopkins wants only to serve me. That is why he is so near to me."

Service brings the servant into the presence of his master. Those who serve the Lord best fellowship with Him most.

An intellectual life of rationality makes Christianity practical. God has given us a brain and He expects us to use it; to be discerning. The capacity of a human brain is phenomenal. One scientist said of it, "If each of your brain cells were a football, there would be enough balls for every amateur and professional game until the year 2373198. Yet no one could play, for the playing filled -- indeed, the entire globe -- would be 27 feet deep in pigskins." Within this grey matter, choices of eternal consequence are made. This is "Control Central's" domed stadium for our real self. We are not necessarily what we think we are; rather what we think, we are. If we consent to God's will, He so identifies Himself with the resulting thoughts and aims as to enfold His power into our actions. At this depth of commitment and obedience, we are carrying out as our own impulses His will. When a logical choice to serve Christ as Master is made, a lifestyle of service is a natural result. A third class mind is only happy when thinking with the majority. A second class mind is only happy when thinking with the minority. A first class mind is only happy when thinking with the mind of Christ.

Second and third class minds act as though the good life is the glandular life. Actions and choices are made on the bases of glandular drives, emotional impulses, and basal appetites. A carnal concept of life results. Like an animal in heat that abandons all survival instincts making itself vulnerable to the hunter, these persons have become prey to "mammon" masquerading as the god of all things good. An intellectual life of rationality exposes this poisoned philosophy as self-delusion resulting in self-destruction.

Our opinions help determine our attitudes, therefore, they must be based on proper information. There is a basic difference in an opinion and an attitude. An opinion is cognitive, that is, based on what is perceived as knowledge. An attitude involves cognitive insight plus an emotion coupled with an action.

Judges render opinions. Their decisions are to be based on knowledge and not swayed by emotions. An opinion may be based on what is perceived as true rather than actual true. Upon learning correct facts on the subject, the opinion can be changed. An attitude may be so ingrained that the emotion doesn't change in light of the new truth. For example, a person may have a bad attitude toward a person based on what is perceived as true about that individual. A friend may share corrected insight forcing a change of opinion, but the emotion supporting the attitude might be so deep that it doesn't change and the same conduct is maintained in the relationship. Thus, the emotion and action don't change. Because of emotional involvement, attitudes are more obstinate. That can be good or bad depending on what they relate to.

If we are to have an intellectual life of rationality, we must have opinions based on Bible truths. Old opinions might have to be changed as a result of a new Bible orientation. Rationality would demand that we show a change of attitude also. Integrity demands that we be willing to change our opinions based on new evidence from God's

Word. Christian maturity can then help us change our attitudes to coincide with new opinions growing out of fresh insight from Scripture. This makes for sagaciousness.

Secular twilight is not the setting in which to make a rational decision. Broad open uplands of God's Word bathed in the sunlight of heaven's love is where choices should be made.

Most people intend to make a decision choosing Christ as Master. A major trap exists in which many mistaken persons are ensnared. It is called "deferred payment". It is the buy now and pay later syndrome. Certain habits are perpetuated with a knowledge that they will cause broken health in the future. People eat wrong today with an awareness they will have clogged arteries tomorrow. Some smoke fully aware that in the future it will cause lung cancer. The pleasures of today are enjoyed at the expense of suffering tomorrow. There is nothing rational about this. Similarly, there are persons who reject Christ as Master today based on emotional impulses and physical pleasures. Their ultimate intent is to avoid deferred payment by making a delayed decision. Because of the "X-factor", that unknown called "the time of death", a decision to delay is a "NO" response to Christ. That is not intellectually rational.

No profession of love of God with all your heart relieves you of the responsibility of loving Him with your head: your wisdom, knowledge, and reason. By that degree to which you remain ignorant of what you could know about God, you are performing a disservice. You are to study to show yourself approved unto Him. Failure to do so is a failure in service.

Knowledge has been defined as the ability to take things apart, while wisdom is the ability to put things together. Spiritual knowledge is awareness of what is taught in God's Word. Wisdom is the ability to make a practical application of it.

The mind is more composed and controlled than the heart, the emotions. We are to investigate, examine, and ultimately approve or disapprove of things considered. After such rational evaluation of a matter, that which is approved becomes a conviction. Thereafter, a decision doesn't have to be made on that subject. It is then only necessary to execute according to the conviction. For that reason, a Biblically enlightened mind is necessary.

Ageless insight is offered by James in his epistle. He wrote: "If any of you lack wisdom, let him ask of God, that gives to all men liberally, and without reproach, and it will be given him" (James 1:5). Literally, this means ask God for wisdom and He won't make you feel foolish for asking; He will give it.

"If" doesn't imply some do and some don't need wisdom. It is first class condition meaning it is an assumed reality, a standing fact. Therefore, prayer for wisdom is appropriate. This wisdom is moral discernment that enables a believer to assess what appears to be an opportunity of service. Sometimes what looks like a good thing to be done would handicap the one on whose behalf it is done.

Jonathan Winters, the noted comedian, tells of asking for a $5.00 a week raise as a young radio announcer in Des Moines, Iowa. He was declined. Later in retrospect he realized that if he had gotten that raise he would have been content to stay there and make spot announcements the rest of his life. That which appeared to be a good thing would have been bad for him.

Emotionally led, well intended believers, can handicap persons by performing a service for them which is unbiblical. Intellectually, it is obvious that to do for persons what they need motivation to do for themselves is unfair. Emotionally the apparent, immediate condition might prompt a service which would be to the recipient's detriment. Intellectual rationality based on Scripture must be employed.

A wealthy brother-in-law refused once again to financially rescue the needy husband of his sister. This seems heartless at first. In reality, it had been done several times before and the brother-in-law had become dependent. Something better than a dole was offered. A generous offer was made to spend as much time as necessary to teach the needy relative Bible financial principles and how to apply them in managing what he had. The offer was declined. An emotional response would have given the money again and again. However, for the sake of the one mismanaging his resources the intellectual rational thing was done. In similar cases we must "ask God" because wisdom is needed.

"Let him ask God" reveals God to be the ultimate source of wisdom. This statement does not just give permission. It is a stated duty. Being in the perfect tense, it means keep on asking. It is God's nature to give continually. If we dare ask "it shall be given..."

In order to be able to make a determination as to whether a particular service would be a help or handicap, Solomon's wisdom needs to be applied. "Trust in the Lord with all your heart, and lean not on your own understanding. In all your ways acknowledge Him, and he shall direct thy paths" (Proverbs 3: 5,6).

We were created to serve the Lord. "Mammon" was created to serve us. We are not to invert this and expect the Lord to serve us while we serve mammon. Christ humbled Himself and became an obedient servant, not that we might order Him around, but that we might follow His example. He always used mammon for the welfare of others. Any rational mind counts the cost of a decision. Mammon is a gilded toy that won't work. Christ makes a loving Master enabling life to work for you. Now count the cost of serving each. Make sure your choice is intellectually rational.

There is an old proverb which states: "A man can't carry two melons in one hand at the same time". You cannot serve God and mammon. You can't serve under two flags. James warned us "A double minded man is unstable in all his ways" (James 1: 8).

Joshua, one of God's choice prophets, once challenged his beloved people from the slopes of historic Mt. Ebal. Their state of indecision was as unbecoming of them as it is unworthy of us. His clarion call to chose a master still rings through the passage ways of reason, "Choose you this day whom ye will serve" (Joshua 24: 15).

CHAPTER 4

THE MOTIVATION OF A SERVANT

One of the most enlightened cultures of its time was the Greek world. Few societies have produced as many great philosophers and scientists. Their thirst for knowledge was incessant and their quest for new sources endless.

Christ often taught on the isolated shores of the Sea of Galilee. Doubtless this was His favorite retreat for various reasons. One was the beauty and solitude. There is an ancient saying that God created all the lakes of the world and then selected the most beautiful parts of each to combine in forming the Galilee.

The gently rolling slopes on the western shore, the low clouds coming in off the Mediterranean Sea, and the reflective surface of the lake made it a natural amphitheater. This design made it an acoustically ideal place to speak to large groups outdoors.

It seemed remote from the great cities of Rome, Athens, Corinth, Jerusalem, Damascus, and Cairo. However, there were converging factors that drew a distinct audience to hear anyone speaking there. The hot artisan wells made it a medical center to which persons came from three continents for healing. The caravan routes from Europe, Asia, and Africa converged here also. Among the hearers of any person speaking would be a cross segment of society. That rural cross road was the Grand Central Station of the day.

It would have been from here word of Christ's capacity as a teacher spread to Greece. Evidently, there had been Greeks among an audience addressed by Christ. They, being major merchants and leaders in the medical community, would have cause to come and go through the area. Impressed by His teaching, they took word back to their home land. Excitement over such a teacher prompted a delegation to be appointed to make an overture to Christ to come to Greece and teach. They would have made of Him a teacher among teachers -- a celebrity. He knew that was not His role and the mission for which He had come was nearing fulfillment.

The Greeks, likely Gentile proselytes to Judaism, had come to the Passover feast in Jerusalem. Finding one of Christ's followers,

Philip, to have a Greek name, they felt this a common bond. They approached this disciple who often served as an intermediary saying "Sir, we would see Jesus" (John 12:22). This did not mean they simply wanted to look at Him to observe His appearance. It was a kind expression asking an audience.

Philip shared their desire with Andrew. Together they told Jesus of the interest of the Greeks. There must have been a mood of melancholy in Jesus' voice as He replied, "The hour is come, that the Son of Man should be glorified" (Verse 23). Christ's role as the Suffering Servant was about to be played out on the dramatic stage of Calvary.

There would be no spiritual harvest unless He like a grain of wheat fell to the ground and died. The sequence in nature was enacted in His life as it must be in ours: obedience - death - life. The quest by the Gentile world evidenced the time had come to establish the completion of the gospel and open it to all people.

Jesus did not follow the Greeks. To have done so would have been disobedience to His calling. The option was His and in exercising

His choice He chose to obey. Instead of following the Greeks He turned to His followers and said, "If anyone serves M e, let him follow Me; and where I am, there M y servant be also: If any man serves Me, him will my Father honor" (Verse 26).

Serving Christ involves following Him. Where He was to go in life and in death His followers would be privileged to accompany Him. All who serve with Him will share with Him. Ultimately what is shared is the glory the Father will bestow on those following the Son.

At this point in time, Jesus once more made a choice. He chose the role of a servant rather than a celebrity. Those who follow Him have to choose also. Persons of notoriety are often followers of Jesus. They, as others, can be followers if they place their status at His service to be used by Him. Throughout the New Testament many such persons are noted. In each instance, their glory was in being the servant of Christ not a prima donna. Christ was motivated by His mission. As the Eternal Corn of Wheat, He was soon to be planted. No man would take His life; it would be laid down willfully -- planted, by choice -- His choice. Actually it was not a single choice but multiple choices. The coming of the Greeks gave occasion for this time of choosing as His hour in Gethsemane would offer yet another.

We who follow the train of those who set out in that hour to follow Him in exercising our capacity to say "Yes" to Him increase our capacity to say "No" to the world. A convicted "Yes" empowers a convincing "No".

F.W. Boreham said, "We make our decisions, and then our decisions turn around and make us. "Our hope for eternity hung on Christ's choice. Had He said "Yes" to the Greeks He would have been saying "No" to His mission. His response meant His mission on planet earth was one step closer to fulfillment. The purpose for which He dawned His earth suit of flesh and blood was approaching a climax.

It has been variously stated that motivation is the capacity to carry out the intent of a decision long after the emotion that inspired it has faded. The pre- creation counsel of the Father, Son, and Holy Spirit (Ephesians 1: 4 - 12) designed redemption's plan. Only by completing that plan would Christ's mission be fulfilled. As Christ drew nearer the cross, increasing allurements and distractions crossed His path.

Each diversionary appeal was a "red herring". This term comes from the annals of British law enforcement. Often dogs were used in tracking persons. A fish, the red herring, has such a dominant odor that persons being tracked would tie one on a string and pull it across their trail. An accomplice might drag it some distance. Invariably the scent would overpower that of the person and the dog would be side tracked. As a result the expression, "that's a red herring," came to refer to anything diverting a person from a proper course. In the person of the Greeks, Satan was employing yet another red herring.

Red herrings are common in believers' lives. People searching for a fulfilling life seem to be susceptible to them. Only by knowing life's objective and making a pre-commitment to it can the red herring syndrome be avoided.

Dostoevsky observed, "The ant knows the formula for the anthill. The bee knows the formula for the bee-hive. They do not know the formulas in a human way, but in their own way. Only man does not know his formula." Humanity's formula is not unknown because it was unstated. Repeatedly Christ taught that we serve our way to fulfillment.

More than once after speaking on the "formula" He concluded by saying, "If you know these things, happy are you if you do them". He has made known the formula. Knowing it is not enough. It must be put into operation. It necessitates being a doer, applying the formula, and not just being a student of it. This takes motivation. Step one is to study the formula. It is spelled summarily in the word servanthood. It is clarified by defining the object of service to be the Lord Jesus Christ. That elementally stated is the formula for a full and meaningful life. All options offered are red herrings. Remember, red herrings are overpoweringly attractive options that cause the main object to be missed. They are followed at the personal expense of fulfillment and the kingdom expense of dishonor.

In responding to the overture made by Philip and Andrew, Jesus gives analytical insight into the formula. Observant study of it can enable a person to know it. Only a highly motivated commitment will enable a person to apply it all through life.

Worldly approval, applause, accolades, or acceptance have caused diversion for many seeking celebrity status instead of servanthood.

THE SERVICE OF PASSIONATE DEVOTION

Jesus knew the strongest motivating force in the world to be love. Love and motivation are almost synonyms. Love has one objective: the welfare of the one loved. It releases all secondary efforts to care for themselves. Therefore, inherent in love is its own reward. Knowing this, Jesus sought to engage His followers in a conspiracy of love. His success among those early followers is attested to by the writing by Statius Caecilius of that circa: "They (the Christians) know one another by secret marks and signs, and they love one another almost before they know one another."

A SOURCE OF DEVOTION

There is a land of the fulfilled and a land of the unfulfilled. Servanthood is the only bridge between the two. Love is the only force strong enough to adequately motivate a person to walk that bridge.

Love for Jesus finds its strength in its object. He did not seek love and devotion to principles, but to Himself. Establishment of this love relationship has been initiated by Him. It must be consummated by us. Once it is, then His motivating power flows into the life of the lover. Someone, I know not who, has wisely said, "Our love for Him will not permit us to ask Him for help, if we are not making any effort; for strength, if we have strength we are not using; for guidance, if we ignore guidance we already have; for forgiveness, if we continue to hate someone; for mercy, if we intend no expression of it."

Love is not just something you feel, it's something you do. Jesus said, "If you love Me keep My commandments" (John 14:15). Then He played the flip side of that truth, "He who does not love Me does not keep My words" (John 14: 24). This makes it self-evident: He who loves Jesus keeps His commandments, he does His will. He who keeps His commandments loves Him. Obedience is the issue. Therefore, if you love Him do something about it. Be useful, follow His example. Simple sentiment or erratic emotion is not enough. Obedience is the issue in servanthood. Obedience was the means by which the Son showed His love for the Father. It is our way to show our obedience for the Son. What price are you willing to pay to obey?

In Austin, Texas, I dined with a man who had given over $5,000,000 the year before to commendable causes. Knowing this to be a regular thing with him, I thought it a good opportunity to ask his opinion regarding new tax laws. A change in the laws made it less advantageous to gain deductions by giving, so I asked if he thought the new law would adversely affect giving. Dick responded, "If a person doesn't have it in his heart to give, no law will motivate him to give. If a person has it in his heart to give, no law will keep him from giving."

A young summer student missionary after returning from an impoverished third world country said to me: "If we can't give out of the abundance we have been given -- who needs the missionary?"

The summer missionary said in effect God has given the American Christian community the resources. In summary, Dick said the issue is not what is in our bank account but in our heart. Love for Christ motivates persons to serve Him with their substance.

Jesus said "He that loves his own life will lose it." The direct reference is to the eternal destiny of the soul. Accompanying that are associated losses. Greed is an effective red herring. It has been the diversion causing Christians to lose more money in get-rich-quick schemes than has been given to the cause of Christ.

Christ spoke often on matters of economics. A cardinal principle was stated by Him when He observed that where a man's heart was there his treasure would also be (Matthew 6:21). Again the controlling factor is love.

A SECRET OF DISASTER

Balance in the teachings of Christ is His hallmark. As love for Him is seen to be an energizing force, so inordinate self-love is known to be destructive. He compassionately warned of the impending dangers for one who "loves his life" (Verse 25). Love seeks one thing only: the good of the one loved. When that object is self that makes for a tight little world.

Watchman Nee, a Chinese pastor, was threatened by his Communist captors in attempt to get him to repudiate his faith. They warned that if he did not rescind his witness his arms would be cut off. In the city square, before a sea of people, he was forced to kneel and place both arms on a block where they were chopped off at the elbow. He staggered to his feet and lifted his bleeding stubs to heaven and prayed, "Thank you, Lord, that I can gladly give my hands in sacrifice to you."

Had Watchman Nee loved his hands more than he loved Jesus he would have saved his hands and lost his witness, his reputation as a faithful servant.

Logic forces the question, "Do you love Jesus enough to sacrifice your hands for Him?" That is to give them whether severed or functional? Do you love Him enough to give Him your broken or diseased body as a witness? Do you love Him enough to give Him your strong healthy body for His use? True love doesn't have a happy ending. As a matter of fact, it doesn't have an ending.

There are many persons devoted to good causes; but few devoted to Jesus. Jesus tipped us off to the conduct of those following Him for what they get out of it rather than what they can put in. Using an analogy of a shepherd, He said that when a wolf comes "He that is a hireling...flees" (John 10:12). Such a professional shepherd, feeling no devotion, would not extend himself on behalf of sheep that were not his own. Loving his own life, he would willingly sacrifice the sheep for his own welfare. The Biblical character Demas is illustrative of this. Of him the sad epitaph lingers "Demas has forsaken me having loved this present world more."

THE SPRING OF DIRECTION

"Follow me," said Jesus (John 12:26). That is spelled
C H A R G E !

We are not to take counsel of our own cravings, but follow His command. Obedience to Him is at once challenging and comforting. Life in Christ is given direction and marked by purpose. Obedience leaves no one idle or bored. There is always a fresh and demanding challenge. A life is complete in proportion to the extent to which it expresses the full intent of our Lord. At first, following Him may take a conscious effort. Growth in grace and knowledge makes it more spontaneous. When fellowship with Christ matures to become reflexive it is most rewarding. It is imperative that we fix our mind on the fact our purpose is to follow Him. In the heat of spiritual warfare, courage is gained by remembering Who you are following. When you are up to your armpits in alligators, you might forget your objective is to drain the swamp, if you are not devoted to the cause.

Jesus called us to follow Him in close proximity when He said, "Take up your cross and follow Me" (Matthew 16:24). The Greek word translated "follow" means to follow intimately. It speaks of nearness that would result in the one's following, stepping in the footprint of the one leading the instant the leader's foot is removed from its track. Following this closely, there is not room for two crosses. Therefore, it being our cross we are called to take up, it becomes evident whose cross Christ was bearing -- ours.

This is no mundane appeal to come enjoy a perpetual euphoric trip, a life-long emotional fling, or engagement in elongated elation. This is once again an invitation to become involved in the natural sequence of following: obedience -- death -- life. Crosses were for executions. No person who loves his own life takes up his cross at the expense of his own life. Only loving obedience to the Lord motivates such behavior.

THE SOCIETY OF PERSONAL DEDICATION

The Society of Servants, the Royal Order of the Towel, is a fulfilled fellowship. They, the servants, are gratified when He, the Lord, is glorified.

FRUITFULNESS OF FRIENDSHIP

Friendship results in fruitfulness. The key word is "servant" as used by our Lord. He said, "where I am, there shall also my servant be" (John 12: 26). That is true in time and for eternity. He has promised, in leaving earth, that He would prepare a place for His followers that where He is there they shall be also (John 14: 2, 3). The argument now moves from the greater to the lesser. If He has already provided for our greatest need, an eternal heavenly home, will He not provide for us as we follow Him thereto?

One elderly Christian lady was mocked by skeptical youths who asked her what she would do if she got to heaven and was not admitted. She said, "I would just walk around the outside shouting of the blessings I had just in getting there." Every child of God should have that spirit because all the way to heaven is heaven even though it might not be heavenly.

Christ meets us at the crossroads of life and shows us which way to go by walking with us. That fellowship sustains even if the pilgrimage goes through the valley of the shadow of death. It is the companion, not the country, that makes the journey. The nature of things around us may tend to make us disloyal. Fellowship with Christ makes us loyal servants.

A young student from mainland China was sent to America to attend the University of Texas. This Communist youth got lost and confused in the Dallas airport. He approached several people and in his broken English asked, "Are you a Christian?" Several persons answered, "no," though they didn't speak a word. Their actions spoke for them. He approached a business man with the enquiry. Warmly, the executive responded, "Yes, how may I serve you". The youth explained his confusion and need for aid in finding his way through the terminal to catch his flight to Austin. "Austin is my home. I am on my way there now. Come with me and I will help you," said the new American friend. As they waited at the gate for their flight, the business man inquired why he had been asked if he were a Christian. The student explained that an older friend from China had attended school at UT.

Upon learning the youth was coming to America, he told him that if he had a need to find a Christian and he would help him.

The root of that help was even more specifically identified when the business man invited the student to attend his church, Hyde Park Baptist. In amazement, the youth told of how his older friend had attended that church as a student to develop the best of friends. That Chinese lad was saying, "Sir, I would see Jesus".

Assurance must have been ignited in that youthful oriental mind when he heard, "Yes, how may I serve you?" Much of the world is awaiting that answer to their unasked question. Such an answer reveals the respondent to be a follower of the Lord. It is an instantaneous witness, a bridge of friendship from Jesus to the world.

FULLNESS OF FELLOWSHIP

Joy is to be found in the land of "where I am." His presence, not the place, is important. In the first chapter of the Revelation, Christ is depicted as standing in the midst of seven golden candlesticks. The candlesticks are the churches. Where is Christ? Positionally, He is already at the right hand of the Father. Experientially, He is always in the midst of the candlesticks, His servants.

"Where I am" land offers no immunity from insult and injury. To love others is to be vulnerable. If you seek to serve others in Jesus' name, you will be used. C.S. Lewis, wrote of this in his work entitled "The Four Loves": "To love at all is to be vulnerable. Love anything, and your heart will certainly be wrung out and possibly broken. If you want to make sure of keeping it intact, you must give your heart to no one, not even to an animal. Wrap it carefully round with hobbies and little luxuries; avoid all entanglements; lock it up safe in the casket or coffin of your selfishness. But in that casket -- safe, dark, motionless, and airless -- it will change. It will not be broken; it will become unbreakable, impenetrable, irredeemable...The only place outside Heaven where you can be perfectly safe from all the dangers ... of love is Hell."

Irony of ironies is there is no fellowship in Hell. That which makes a hell of hell is the absence of the loving fellowship of the Lord. Hell is the homeland of those disobedient to our loving Lord.

There those who have refused to serve the Lord will serve with their lord Lucifer. No man can serve two masters, but every man must serve one. With the choice of the one goes the company that one keeps.

FULFILLMENT OF FAITHFULNESS

Jesus said of those who obey Him in faithful service "him will my Father honor" (John 12: 26). This provision applies to time and eternity.

Some years ago in Elko, Nevada, there lived a successful young, cynical business man. He was bitter, critical, and skeptical. One day a minister asked him, "Are you a Christian?" It angered John Randolph, but he could not forget the question or deny the awful negative answer. It lead to his eventual conversion. As he and his wife grew in faithful service they studied the Bible. This prompted them to ask their pastor, "What is this we hear about the Bible teaching tithing?" Timorously, the pastor assured them it did. Randolph replied, "Very well, we'll do it". A second question, "Someone told us we are to witness to others. Are we?" Again the pastor swallowed deep and answered, "Yes."

"Ok," said Randolph, "we will". Several such diagnostic questions regarding the Christian faith followed and John Randolph responded compliantly to each.

Little wonder that a few years later when the pastor left that church the Lord honored John Randolph by the people's insisting that he become their pastor. Having been faithful in that which was least, the Lord made him responsible for that which was greater. The Father honored him.

Life's greatest reward for a seed is that it might reproduce. Years ago a crusty old sergeant in the Highland Regiment in Egypt was saved. In recounting his conversion, he told how the obedient faith of a private on Malta was used of the Lord to influence him. One night the sergeant saw the private kneeling to pray beside his bunk which was next to the sergeant's. It angered the officer who was in the process of removing his boot. In a rage he struck the private in the head with his boot. After a moment of recovery, the private resumed his prayer. The next morning the sergeant's boots were polished. This compassionate gesture reached the heart of the offender. The Father honored the obedient act of servitude and salvation was the crown.

In Coventry, England, I saw depicted the ultimate victory with which the Father will honor those faithful to His Son. Coventry's magnificent old Cathedral was destroyed by Nazi bombs. Lovingly the people of the city built a new one in conjunction with the standing ruins. Just outside the entrance to the ornate new facility there is a striking larger-than-life sculpture. It depicts Michael, the arch angel, spear in hand, poised triumphantly over a prostrated, manacled dragon. Pictured is our honor, the joy of being a part of the ultimate victory through Christ.

THE SEAL OF PERFECT DISCIPLINE

No person is truly free if undisciplined. Great discipline is needed by a musician in order to best be able to improvise. Discipline is required for an athlete to innovate. Greater discipline is required by a servant to be able to render spontaneous service. The more nearly perfect the discipline the more joyous the service.

THE DRILL OF PURITY

Those who serve Christ best do so out of a pure heart. There is a difference in innocence and purity. An infant is innocent but a forgiven Christian is pure. It is a dangerous thing to be close to a holy thing and not be pure. In ordering His people to follow the ark into the Land of Promise, God warned them to keep their distance. Purity in following the Lord is no less essential for His servants. By example, a pure life exerts an influence second in power only to the power of God. It is purity, not pleasure, that motivates the doer and the recipient.

Does it ever seem you just can't work up fervent love for your brothers and sisters? Are you occasionally challenged by a lack of emotional thrill over rendering some laborious service in the name of the Lord? Even if it is rare, the infrequent absence of this religious emotion is bewildering to some. Extreme reactions all the way to "Am I really saved?" result. Take heart! You can move from the dark shadow of doubt into the refreshing light of reality if you know there are two aspects to love. One is feeling. The other an act of the will. God does not intend His people to be yo-yos on the strings of their emotions. Stability occurs when emotional highs are accepted as the gravy resulting from willful cooking of the meat. It is our will that must remain as a constant chef.

Benard of Clairvaux in asking and answering his own question explains for us why we must maintain consistent love resulting in obedience. "Why," he asks, "should we love God? Because He is God". No other explanation is needed; no emotion required. Our will takes us where our emotions fear to go.

THE DUTY OF PATIENCE

Fundamental to the word "serve" is patience. To serve and keep on serving requires patience. For this reason our Lord asks no one to follow Him who is not His servant.

Life on death row takes patience. William Moore lives on death row in Jackson, Georgia. What resulted in that being his residence was tragic and grievous. William knows only one vehicle, a hearse, will take him from this prison. Therefore, his late developing faith in Christ isn't a ploy for a reprieve. Recently he wrote me, "Death row is common in the world, for all live on it until Christ translates them to life row". With that mind set William and others there serve the Lord patiently by maintaining a prayer ministry for persons in and out of prison.

In a Siberian cell another life wasted away. Pitirim Sorokin spent four years on death row in Russia. He penned these words: "Whatever may happen in the future I know that I have learned three things which remain forever convictions of my heart as well as my mind. Life, even the hardest life, is the most beautiful, wonderful, miraculous treasure in the world...fulfillment of duty is another marvelous thing making life happy. This is my second conviction. My third is that cruelty, hatred, violence, and injustice never can and never will be able to create...The only way...is the royal road of all-giving creative love, not only preached, but consistently practiced".

Consistency is a virtue of our Lord needed in His servants. In Him there is no caprice or changeableness. Among His closest followers were those who betrayed Him, forsook him, and denied

Him. In it all He remained consistent. Pain, injury, insult, nor affront caused Him to waver.

With the visit by the Greeks came another allurement. In the wake of their approval and appeal, He remained consistent. There was no wavering. They offered a new option to His servanthood. It was celebrity status. Attentiveness and attention awaited in their center of culture. He remained consistent.

People are inclined to make short term commitments. It is estimated that annually approximately 52 percent of the population makes a New Year's resolution. A poll revealed that 38 percent of those who make resolutions are able to abide by them for only seven days; 33 percent keep them for a few weeks; 17 percent honor their new promises for several months; and only 12 percent effectively implement resolutions that make a lasting positive change.

One of the most effective helps for keeping a commitment is to announce it. Research has demonstrated that you are more likely to keep resolutions if you tell other people about them. One research study found that 86 percent of the participants who published their goals achieved them. On the other hand, only 14 percent to those who kept their resolutions secret were able to accomplish them.

In calling you to serve Him, our Lord has not asked you to join the Secret Service. He desires demonstrable voluntary enlistment in public service. It is kind of difficult to hide a cross. If you dare take it up, it will be public.

There are no honorary positions available in His service corps though it is an honor to serve.

Listen as the world still entreats, "We would see Jesus." Will you so serve Him as to show them?

CHAPTER 5

THE MODEL OF A SERVANT

There is a clinic in progress involving a lecture and a demonstration. The subject: SERVANTHOOD. The instructor: The archetype of a servant Himself, Jesus Christ. Let's slip in the back door to listen and observe.

First, our understanding of what happens in this room will be greatly enhanced if we know a bit of the background. It is the evening before Jesus fulfills His ultimate role as the Suffering Servant. The hour of His agony is at hand. He is fully aware that tomorrow He will be executed by crucifixion. In doing so He will serve all mankind by providing for the forgiveness of sin. For this purpose He came into the world.

He and His close friends have gathered to celebrate the ancient right of Passover. For centuries their ancestors have traditionally gathered to commemorate Jehovah's deliverance of their predecessors from slavery in Egypt. Every act and every element is symbolically significant.

However, there is a custom of their period which Jesus employs to communicate a new spirit. Doctrine without devotion, custom without commitment, and symbolism without substance only makes for dry bones. A new breath of meaning is about to be breathed into life for those who follow Christ after this night.

Let's enter quietly into the room to observe and listen. Before entering spiritually prepare yourself by resolving to become a practitioner of what is being taught by practice and precept. This is a "how-to clinic" for future servants.

Jesus is the host. All elements are prepared and the table set. The twelve apostles have bathed and groomed for this special event. Roadways of the era were dusty and sanitation in the cobblestone streets was nil. Animals traveled the same streets as humans. Often excrement stayed in the street for days. Walking in a crowd inevitably resulted in sandal-shod persons having dirty feet after only a short walk. With an awareness of this, hosts always had a servant who would wash the feet of guests. They, having bathed before a feast, were then clean all over after the foot washing.

Jesus took upon Himself the form of a servant. He humbled Himself, took a towel, a basin of water, and began washing the disciples' feet. Their Master and Teacher was giving an object lesson never to be forgotten. It was not an act or a new ceremony, but an attitude and spirit. He Who was greatest was serving in the role of the lesser. He was the servant. As such He demonstrated in the upper room what He taught in the open market: "...he that is greatest among you shall be your servant" (Matthew 23:11). He was now visualizing what He had vocalized.

A simple statement of fact reveals a significant principle. He "rose from supper, and laid aside his garments; and took a towel, and girded Himself" (John 13: 4). That single sentence describing His physical conduct is a summary of His advent and adventure of earth. He "laid aside his garments," that is, He "being in the form of God, thought it not robbery to be equal with God: But made himself of no reputation" (Philippians 2: 6, 7). He "took a towel," meaning He "took upon him the form of a servant" (Philippians 2: 7). Then He "girded himself," that is

He "being found in fashion as a man, he humbled himself, and became obedient unto death, even the death of the cross" (Philippians 2: 8).

Believing Analogia Scriptura, that is, the Scripture is always analogous to itself, it never contradicts itself, this analogy becomes even more clear.

JESUS SHOWED COMMITMENT

There is a low tone, high intensity argument going on among the disciples as Christ quietly pours a basin of water.

For three years the twelve have been following Christ. They have had the joy of observing and the blessing of hearing Him. They of all people were privileged to be His confidants. He was their mentor. Once they gathered in the upper room it became apparent they had listened, but not learned.

Dr. Luke says "there was also a strife among them, which of them should be accounted the greatest" (Luke 22: 24). They were seeking celebrity status. For days they had heard the increased talk about Christ as a dynamic potential leader. Even His enemies knew of His ability as a leader. As a result, that was a heady group assembled for the last supper with their tutor. Each was jockeying for position. The "Hosannas" of the street were still ringing in the corridors of their minds. They loved praise even if it were proxy praise. They were showing a "groupie" mentality. As "hangers-on" they wanted the benefits of Christ's super star status.

Most persons join churches for all the right reasons. Most ministers seek to serve the Lord only because of His divine calling. However, there are exceptions to both of these principles. Some persons join churches because in their eyes it is an accepted part of the community and in their thought represents success. By association they hope to garner a bit of its glow. Some persons enter the ministry because "Jesus sells." Knowing of Christ's popularity among the group constituting the church they want to gain popularity with the mass by identity with the object of the public's love. Such groups are seeking substitutionary celebrity status. Persons in both of these groups may for a season render admirable service in the energy of the flesh. Being improperly motivated, they eventually falter and become unfaithful.

Privately, the mother of James and John, an earthly aunt of Jesus, had tried to gain a family favor by asking that her boys be allowed to sit on his right and left in His kingdom. If they couldn't be the super star, she wanted them to bask in His glow. Celebrity status by association was okay with her.

The other disciples were incensed by this underhanded favor seeking. They weren't indignant because she tried it, but because she beat their own little Jewish mothers to the point. They came to the upper room seeking status, but are about to get a never to be forgotten lesson on servanthood.

They lacked a commitment to Christ's principles and practices. That didn't deter Him from making a commitment to them. As the first order of business He quelled their quarrel by tucking up His robe, taking a towel and a basin of water, and began washing their feet. That is the job of a servant. Previously, in a more spiritual moment, they had called Him Master and Lord -- appropriately. Now He serves them as their domestic. To wash those odorous dirty feet took commitment. To do it for impudent and arrogant status seekers required greater commitment.

One unwilling to pay the price of humility to be a servant produces mediocre service. True servanthood always exacts a heavy toll on the whole person; the more effective the service, the higher the price to be paid.

Seventeenth-century English Puritan, Richard Baxter, in his work "The Reformed Pastor," wrote that service "must be managed laboriously and diligently, being of such unspeakable consequence to others and to ourselves. We are seeking to uphold the world, to save it from the curse of God, to perfect the creation, to attain the ends of Christ's redemption, to save ourselves and others from damnation, to overcome the devil, and demolish his kingdom, and set up the kingdom of Christ, and attain and help others to the kingdom of glory. And are these works to be done with a careless or a slack hand? Oh see then that this work be done with all your might!"

If we are going to follow our Lord, we too must make an uncompromising commitment. No cost must be spared, no quarter given the adversary, and no compromise made with sin. Would Christ have stooped to wash those crusty feet in a state of self-centered egomania or euphoric self-indulgence? No! Only a combination of love and humility would motivate such action. There are ten different words in the New Testament that speak of commitment. A look at one of them will aid our understanding of what is involved in making a commitment to be the servant of Christ.

This vital word is found in I Peter 4: 19, "Therefore let those who suffer according to the will of God commit their souls to Him in doing good, as to a faithful Creator." The Greek word translated "commit" is PARATITHESTHOSAN. Its root parts are PARA meaning "alongside" and TITHEMI meaning "to lay".

The word was used in several ways. One usage was as a legal term meaning to deposit; to lay down something for safe keeping. In committing to serve Christ, we are investing our lives not in His cause, but in Him. He then pays dividends through us. No reluctance should be shown to do so for we are entrusting ourselves to "a faithful Creator." He is able to keep that which is committed to Him. This should result in confident servants who know they are not dependent upon their own resources, but those of their Master.

No bank can secure a deposit with certainty comparable to that our Lord affords those committed to Him. Vaults fail, alarm systems can be by-passed, and insured deposits can be lost. Not so with our Lord, He keeps that which His servants commit to Him.

A second use of the term relates to laying down something for another as Christ laid down His life for us. Likewise, we are to lay down our lives in service to Him. The recipient of our service might be something more base than an ugly dirty foot. With a fixation of Christ as the one on whose behalf it is done the task becomes a joy. It is as unto the Lord.

Third, there is a form of commitment implied in the use of the word that is difficult. It means to entrust a person to someone else. There are those moments when we have to release a person into the care of our Lord. Death is best responded to in this manner. Any loss in Christ's name can be counted as gain. When a loved one is rolled through the emergency room doors at the hospital and doors are closed, leaving us outside, we have entrusted our beloved to a human doctor. Having done so, why not apply the same principle to our Lord?

As Paul left his friends in Ephesus he said, "And now, brethren, I commend you to God, and to the word of His grace" (Acts 20: 32).

If we make a commitment of this nature to Christ we are in His care to do His bidding. Thereafter, we are under orders. As with a slave, the issue is simply ownership. We are then dependent upon Him for protection and provision. In return we await His order. Our only proper response is "Yes, Lord," to His every wish.

The Apostle Paul reminded us as he did his young aspirant Timothy of the extent of such commitment: "For to this end we both labor and suffer reproach, because we trust in the living God..." (I Timothy 4: 10). Failure to count the cost of commitment often consequents in short-term faithfulness. There is a price to be paid. "Labor" translates KOPIAO which means to work to the point of weariness. "Suffer reproach" translates AGONIZOMAI which means to agonize in a struggle.

Now lest someone should think the toll to be paid for serving the Lord is grievous and the life conformed to evil an easy one consider this: "...as ye have yielded your members servants to uncleanness and to iniquity unto iniquity; even so now yield your members servants to righteousness unto holiness. For when ye were servants of sin, ye were free from righteousness. What fruit had ye then in those things whereof ye are now ashamed? for the end of those things is death.

I speak in human terms because of the weakness of your flesh. For just as you presented your members as slaves of uncleanness, and lawlessness leading to more lawlessness, so now present your members as slaves of righteousness for holiness. For when you were slaves of sin, you were free in regard to righteousness. What fruit did you have then in the things which you are now ashamed? For the end of those things is death?" Romans 6: 19 - 22).

Never judge a journey by its route alone. Follow the trail until you find where it ends. A fact can be learned one of two ways:

experientially or academically. If we academically learn the ends of the routes of being "servants of uncleanness" and being "servants to righteousness unto holiness" we can spare ourselves much experiential misery. The price to be paid for serving the Lord is worth it.

One admirable thing about the Bible is its honesty, not just its truthfulness. It is honest in telling faithful followers of the Lord that doing so is difficult. There is no way the Bible could be convicted for false advertising. Conversely, society falsely glamorizes and synthesizes pretentious pleasures. However, the world could never afford to be as honest about the end product of its art as the Bible.

The liquor industry can show a striking couple enticing each other with their eyes and having a cool one in a seductive setting. They can't show the end product. They must falsify and lie. They can't take you a few hours later to the morgue and show you the lifeless body picked up off the road because of DUI. They won't take you in the emergency room and show you four broken and bloody bodies of family members in a coma awaiting surgery.

Sin is a sweet suitor, but a cruel mistress. Moses is described as "Choosing rather to suffer affliction with the people of God, than to enjoy the pleasures of sin" (Hebrews 11: 25). Again the honesty of the Bible emerges. There is the clear acknowledgement that sin has pleasure. Some present day saints try to pretend it doesn't. Scripture says yes it does "for a season," that is, for a little while. The Psalmist gives us the option: "You will show me the path of life; in Your presence is fullness of joy; at Your right hand there are pleasures for evermore" (Psalms 16: 11).

Both the path of service of sin and service for our Lord have pleasures. The first offers pleasures that are short lived -- then the unadvertised kickback. The other has pleasures "for evermore"; that is, they last. Every person freely chooses his or her pleasures. In doing so be kind to your tomorrow self.

It is wise to state our commitment, but it is essential to show our commitment as did Christ. In taking the towel to serve, He demonstrated His commitment. The towel, though difficult to dramatize, would be a fitting symbol of Christianity. The cross, the fish, and an assortment of vogue lapel pins are commendable. The towel speaks of the ongoing ministry of service.

In fine fashionable restaurants waiters often stand by with towels draped over their arms waiting to serve. Every believer needs to develop that mental self-image and enact the service resulting.

JESUS SPOKE A COMMAND

Confusion often creeps in at this critical point and diverts some people from Christ's intended objective. Jesus said, "You should do as I have done to you" (John 13: 15). There are those who take Him literally and think His primary lesson was symbolical foot washing. This was more than a mere command to wash feet. That is the easy way out.Several internal things in the text reveal this was not the establishment of an ordinance of foot washing. Jesus said, "A new commandment I give unto you" (Verse 34). Foot washing wasn't new. It was the custom of the day. Had it been a new practice started on this occasion we might have reason to believe this to be a commandment to do it.

If the command had simply related to foot washing He would not have said, "What I am doing you do not now" (Verse 7). They knew full well what He was doing in washing feet. Therefore, He must have been referring to something else.

If His command was mere foot washing He would not have asked, "Do you know what I have done unto you?" (Verse 12). They were experientially familiar with foot washing. He is revealing much more to them than simply how to give a pedicure.

If it were foot washing He was commanding He would not have said, "...you should do as I have done to you" (Verse 15). Were foot washing His command He would have said, "Do what I have done to you."

At various times in history foot washing has been practiced with pride. Various popes of Rome in lavish robes and with bejeweled hands have stepped for a moment out of their opulent quarters and publically ceremoniously washed the feet of selected persons. Martin Luther called such "an abominable papal corruption." The ceremonious literal washing of feet can be a dodge for doing what

Christ was actually teaching. What then is this "new commandment"? What are we to do "as" Jesus did?

The disciples understood foot washing, but their internal dispute over station and rank indicated they didn't understand servanthood. Right in the middle of one of their status fits Jesus drops the bomb of servanthood. What an ego crusher!

In giving this command Jesus was appealing to His followers to set aside rank and show humility. They needed to start where servanthood begins. It begins with a simple three word prayer: "Change, me Lord."

This command goes even a step further. It is an encouragement to assume even the lowest rank for "one another." Anybody would want to serve a king, BUT to serve a serf? That's different.

By now Christ was getting their attention. The lecture and demonstration combined were beginning to capture their imagination. This was a new concept. Class superiority, racial arrogance, social status, economic advantages, educational eminence, and political ascendancy were being canceled in this class on classlessness called "Servanthood".

Take down the sign over the door: "YUPPIES UNITED". Post its replacement: "The Royal Order Of The Towel". Enter here all you who would serve. Have you ever noticed how narrow that door is and how untrafficked the carpet?

Humility is a hard thing to fake consistently. Augustine said, "It was pride that changed angels into devils; it is humility that makes men as angels."

Modern day would-be disciples of Christ like those in that upper room must first become teachable before they can be serviceable. As Christ gradually gained their attention, He was slowly changing their character. Three days later they would stand in awe of Christ's holiness and divine sovereignty. Only then would they realize their own littleness and be willing for their minds to be turned upside down. Then they would become practitioners of what they were being taught in the upper room.

From our vantage point we can see clearly His supernatural God nature. This should motivate us to fall on our faces uttering a holy "Yes, Jesus, what would you have me as your servant do?"

I am convinced that the only proper spirit of a true servant of the Lord is that "He must increase and I must decrease". When the beloved John the Baptist reached this point he was ready to serve His Lord even in the death chamber. When that stage of servanthood is reached then the overflow hides the vessel.

On a cool day in Kansas I stood and watched a wheat field teach humility. As I looked across that vast expanse of wheat, it became apparent that the wheat shafts that held their heads erect were the empty heads. The full heads bowed as in reverent servanthood having produced that for which they were created.

As Christ humbled Himself so we must if we would serve Him. It is, after all, that for which we were recreated.

The driving force behind humble service is well defined by Christ in His upstairs classroom. He stated it is a "commandment." The term was often used for a military order coming from a commanding officer. Therefore, what follows comes to us as His enlisted officers. A hush must have fallen over the squabbling disciples and their aspirations as celebrities faded as Christ asserts, "A new commandment I give to you, that you love one another; as I have loved you, that you also love one another. By this shall all men know that you are My disciples, if you have love one to another" (John 13: 34, 35).

Christ knew human nature. Love says, "I appreciate you." Philosopher/psychologist, Will James, wrote a classical work entitled "Principles of Psychology." It is still a primary reference work in the field. Later he admitted "an immense omission" in this pioneer work. He wrote, "The deepest principle of human nature is the craving to be appreciated." His regret was that he had not dealt with it in his book. Tragically many fail to deal with in their daily lives. Status aspirants have little time to appreciate others while seeking it personally. Christ calls upon us to acclaim others without seeking acclaim. Those who forget themselves are best remembered by others. When we love others their welfare, not our interest, is foremost in our attitudes and actions.

Servants who love share with others. In the northern California city of Tiburon there is a distinctive hospital that uses this philosophy as part of its treatment. The hospital, called "The Center for Attitude Healing," (what a perfect name for a church) specializes in children suffering from traumatic diseases or disabling accidents. In addition to superb medical treatment this hospital adds a plus in healing. Patients are encouraged to participate in their own healing and that of others. This has produced a beautiful community of compassionate love.

Staffers stress to the children that they can triumph over their adversities. An often repeated theme is: "If you can help somebody else, you're not disabled."

If you were to consider the disabling condition of 13 year old Joe, a patient at the center, you might at first glance think he is beyond recovery. Having been run over by a tractor, he was almost completely paralyzed. Joe was blind, without speech, and could use only one arm. He was still in a state of hostility resulting in depression causing him to refuse to respond to therapy.

Just a few beds away was a two-year old boy suffering from a brain irritation. As a result the child cried hour after hour.

Joe's mother reflected on his helpless state and seemingly hopeless condition and remembered those words, "If you can help somebody else, you're not disabled." Gingerly she picked up the infant and lovingly placed him in the bed beside Joe with his little head resting on Joe's arm. Instantly Joe stiffened with surprise. At first he was so rigid with tension that he quivered. Ever so slowly Joe moved his one functional arm up and began to stroke the child very gently. Almost immediately the child stopped crying. The abated agitation caused by the crying aided the healing of the brain irritation.

Oh, yes, Joe! He is living proof that the best way to get out of your own adversity is to reach out to someone in his adversity. Soon after developing a caring relationship with the two-year old, Joe's depression began to come under control. He began to talk and soon was willing to start therapy to walk.

Those who love care and share. Joe should mirror all of us. There are those needing our stroking. A simple stroke, be it physically or verbally, can help healing -- our own and that of others. Who are we to serve? Edna St. Vincent Millay defines our sphere of service in this line: "The world stands out on either side no wider than the heart is wide." Followers of our Lord should be big hearted. Jesus said to His followers in their myopic moment of envisioned star status: "You call me Master and Lord: and you say well; for so am I" (John 13: 13). "Master" means one from whom to learn. Lord" means one to follow.

Listen to His lecture. Look at His example. It is not enough just to learn -- we must practice. Gird up your loins. Get your towel. It is time to go to work serving in love. We are to learn from His lecture and follow His example. In essence Christ was saying, "I have taught you humility and love, now follow my example -- serve."

One of my sons-in-law, Dr. Roger Hill, said in medical school there was a descriptive saying regarding medical practices: "You see one, you do one, you teach one." Having heard and seen Jesus in action as a servant in the upper room it is time to move to the "do one" stage.

JESUS STRESSED CLEANSING

Christ's physical act of washing feet depicts a spiritual sequel. He said, "He who is bathed needs only to wash his feet, but is completely clean...." (Vs. 10). Freely transliterated that teaches a great truth. The essence of the teaching is thus distilled. "Since you took a bath before coming to the upper room you have gotten your feet dirty walking in the dust and filth of the street. Your body is clean, but your feet dirty. If you will wash your feet, you will once again be clean all over. You only need to wash your feet, not your body."

Impulsive Peter said, "Lord, not my feet only, but also my hands and my head" (Verse 9). That wasn't necessary physically. Neither is the spiritual parallel necessary. They didn't need to take another bath. When Christians sin they don't need to be "saved again". They need spiritual cleansing resulting in renewal. Jesus used two words in verse ten for wash. He said, "He that is washed (LOUO) needs not save to wash (NIPTO) his feet..." The first meant to take a complete bath. The other means to rinse off part of the body. The first (LOUO) has its spiritual equivalent in salvation at which time we are totally forgiven and cleansed. However, after salvation believers walk in a spiritually defiling world and need cleansing; the spiritual equivalent to washing (NIPTO) the feet. Sin in the life of a Christian does not rob that one of salvation. It does rob such a one of the joy of salvation and clouds an effective witness. It is a sure stopper of service. At this point spiritual cleansing is needed. I John 1:9 is a short course in spiritual cleansing: "If we confess our sins, He is faithful and just to forgive us our sins, and to cleanse us from all unrighteousness." "If" means this action is optional. It is a matter of the will. "We" means it is personal and no one can do it for us. "Confess" means to agree with God about it. That is, to name it as sin and turn from it. "He is faithful" acknowledges His unfailing consistency in forgiving repentant person. He will do it every time -- every time. "And just" is a statement focusing not only on His authority to do so, but also stressing His provision of the means for such just acquittal.

"To forgive us our sins" references to our initial salvation. This is equivalent to the LOUO act in the upper room.

"To cleanse us from all unrighteousness" pertains to pardoning the sins of a Christian committed after salvation. The word "unrighteousness," that is, negative or minus righteousness, is a reference to the sins of a Christian. He forgives them all. This is comparable to the NIPTO experience in the upper room.

For a servant of our Lord to be serviceable this is essential. Our Lord will use an old vessel, a broken vessel, and ugly vessel, BUT He won't use a dirty vessel. Spiritual cleansing is preparatory to proper service.

The hour is late. The demonstration complete for the moment and the lecture about to end. Still Christ wants to impress upon His ambitious class the inherent blessing of following His example as servants. "If you know these things," He says, "happy are you if ye do them" (Verse17).

In his commentary on John, William Hendriksen makes the following observation. "'If you know these things,' according to the context Hr means, If you know that (a.) He who is Lord and Teacher is willing to minister to the needs of those who are his subjects and pupils, even though in doing so He has to stoop very low; and if you know that (b.) all the more, those who were thus benefited should be willing to serve one another in humility of spirit; if you know these things, blessed are you if you do them.

The word Jesus used that is translated "happy" means superlatively blessed, most blessed. God smiles on those who constantly serve humbly in love. Inevitably this quality will color the heart with joy.

A chief export of hell is superficial happiness without holiness. Often those who want happiness most are those living in such a way as to make it impossible. Seeking happiness in the context of a godless life is like looking for a termite in a steel mill.

Do you want happiness? It is inherent in serving. You can serve yourself to happiness. You can't help yourself to happiness but by helping others you serve yourself to it. According to Christ the beautiful by-product of service by a clean servant is happiness. To be holy is to be happy. To be sanctified is to be satisfied. To be committed is to be contented.

Happiness begins with a commitment such as Jesus patterned for us. By making such a commitment you have the blessings inherent therein. Therefore, make it and get on with the serving. Never put off till tomorrow what you can do today. You might enjoy it so much today you will want to do it again tomorrow.

The eminence of the hour of His betrayal and the associated anguish of denial weighed heavily on Jesus. Yet, He lost not the opportunity to impart this reminder: "The servant is not greater than his master; nor is he who is sent greater than he who sent him" (John 13:16).

We are exhorted to do as Christ has done. Therefore, if you do not consider yourself superior to our Lord take upon your arm the towel of a servant and attend others as His servant. As He has served us we are to serve Him. There is a close connection between a servant and his "Lord and Master." All that the Son was to the Father we are to be to Him. All that the Father was to the Son He will be to us. Membership to the "Royal Order of the Towel" is now open.

The Clinic is closed. The clinicians leave with the words of Jesus ringing in their ears, "do as I have done to you."

CHAPTER 6

THE MENTALITY OF A SERVANT

A servant is a servant regardless of the circumstances. On the evening of His execution, Christ dramatized the role of a servant by washing the feet of the disciples, and then watched the reaction. Upon completing the washing of their feet, Christ broke bread and gave it to His disciples as a reminder of His body soon to be pierced for them. He shared the cup as a crimson graphic of His blood to be shed for them.

Moved by love His candor showed itself once more as He warned of His imminent betrayal. Using an idiom of His day He said, "He who eats bread with me has lifted up his heel against me" (John 13:18). The expression meant "one of you at this table is about to stab me in the back". Condensed: "One of you whom I chose to serve with me is about to disobey me".

John, "leaning back on Jesus' breast, he said to Him, 'Lord, who is it?'" (John 13: 25).

Peter said, "Lord... I will lay down my life for your sake" (John 13: 37).

Judas, "having received the piece of bread, he then went out immediately...." (John 13: 30).

Thomas questioned him in such a manner as to disparage the clarity of His teaching: "... how can we know the way?" (John 14: 5).

Philip implied He had clouded the issue and implored Him, "show us the Father, and it is sufficient for us" (John 14: 8).

The Suffering Servant accepted their actions as a final frustration filter and an occasion for further instruction regarding the mentality of a servant. The corridors of the centuries ring with the truths He taught there. Even more importantly, His responses reveal for all ages the supreme example of a servant. It is willing obedience to the Father that is acceptable; He detests what is coerced or forced; it is a tax and not a tribute. Service must not be extracted, but it must exude as honey from a cone. It must come forth naturally as fragrance from a flower. If a sweet spirit and submissive will is missing, service rendered has no acceptance before a loving and giving God. Like a honey cone pressed and a flower crushed, Jesus was about to render His final faithful obedient service; to give His best, Himself.

Having declared and demonstrated His love for them, Christ moved to establish a test by which they and all who follow Him in whatever period of time might have their love for Him tested. This test is still applicable.

John, commonly accepted as the disciple "whom Jesus loved," later wrote of the upper room episode. Christ's words were kept fresh in his memory by the Holy Spirit. Resultantly, He quoted Christ extensively. In the portion of his gospel dealing with the upper room events, several themes are woven together to form a tapestry of wisdom. For our purpose, focus will be placed on that part of the fabric germane to servanthood. His test to determine whether a person had the mentality of a servant was obedient love. Servanthood is the fruit by which the root of obedient love is clearly revealed. If the root is healthy, the fruit is sure. It is an emphatic identification of a servant mentality just as a fingerprint is of a specific person. Until the turn of the century, fingerprints were not known to be an identifying mark. The distance measured from a person's elbow to the tip of the middle finger was used for identification. In 1904, Scotland Yard in England began using fingerprints for the first time. Fingerprinting rapidly gained popular acceptance as a sure method of identification. Obedient love is even more accurate in identifying a person with the mentality of a servant.

To Christ obedience was always the true test of love. He never hinted that love was simple sentiment or erratic emotion. It is the thread in the fabric of life that never fades no matter how often it is washed in the water of grief and adversity. Love for the Master always reveals itself in obedience. Love and disobedience are self-excluding. To make sure this fact was established Christ stated it two ways.

First, He said, "If you love Me, keep My commandments" (John 14: 15). That is clear enough, but just to make sure there is no misunderstanding He rephrased it: "He who does not love Me does not keep my word...." (John 14: 24). Paraphrased those two statements mean: He who loves me keeps my commandments. He who keeps my commandments loves me. "He" is an emphatic pronoun, thus, it means, "He and he alone is the one loving me."

"Love is the spring of action; therefore, if you love Me do something -- serve Me. Be useful -- follow My example," was the essence of His plaintive plea. Faithful service is the insignia of a loving heart.

Love is known by the action it prompts. This is even true of our Heavenly Father. He loved so He "gave". Lovingly the heavenly heartbeat could not remain garrisoned in the Celestial City. It poured over the ramparts of eternity into the lives of human beings. Personified in Christ, it was demonstrated in an alien environment. Heaven's love embodied in Christ sought ways to express itself toward the unloving, unlovely, and unlovable. Those who received it were transformed by it and became conductants of His love. As Heaven couldn't contain all of His love, so, no life can. Those who become recipients of Christ's love do not become mere repositories of love, but relayers.

Jesus said of those who love Him they will serve Him by keeping His commandments. What did He mean by "keep My commandments"? An expanded translation reveals the meaning more clearly: "If with love that is both intelligent and purposeful you love me, you will accept, obey, and stand guard over the rules which I have laid down for the regulation of your inner attitudes and outer conduct."

He thus allows those who love Him to become the custodians of His love revealed. They are not compelled to serve, but inner love for Him becomes a compulsion that can't be kept from manifesting itself in selfless service. As an air bubble suppressed in a solution of oil can't be kept from rising to the top, so love surfaces as sacrificial service to Him. It is reflexive.

A reflexive action can't be faked or prevented. A sneeze is a reflexive action. When you have to sneeze, you can't keep from it. You may try until you are blue in the face, but you are going to sneeze. You might suppress it for a while and muffle it a bit, but you are going to sneeze. As sure as you sneeze, someone is sure to quote these lines:

I sneezed a sneeze into the air.

It fell to earth I know not where

But fixed and froze, Were the stares of those in whose direction I snooze.

Breathing is a reflexive action. Unless someone calls attention to the fact you are breathing, you simply do it without an awareness. It is natural.

Faithful service is the reflexive action of a heart of love. Opportunities of service are sought. Instinctively, when an opportunity presents itself, the person with a servant mentality responds. For years my beloved dad and mom had an instinct for service opportunities. If they had been asked about their service, they would have been as unaware that they were serving as we normally are of breathing.

Remember Jesus telling of those who visited Him in prison, gave Him food, and clothed Him, and those who had asked, "when?" Their service in His name had been so genuine that they forgot to keep score. This spontaneous action is typical of a person with a servant mentality. He becomes so involved in doing that he doesn't remember to keep a tally of his "brownie points". Completing one joyous opportunity to serve, it is fundamental for them to move to the next.

We who profess to love Christ live under His command to serve. Inspired by His example, we become motivated to comply. Lawyers interpret every event of life through the eyes of the law. Athletes view all of life's experiences from the vantage point of a competitor. Farmers have an agrarian outlook on life. A physicist looks at life from a scientific standpoint. Persons of each of these disciplines and all others who have love for Christ look at life as a series of opportunities to serve their Lord by ministering to others in His name. To "keep" His commandments means three things.

TO ACCEPT

Jesus said, "If any one loves Me, he will keep My word" (John 14: 23). His "word" constitutes all He said. We are not to pick and choose which to accept and obey. The commandments we keep -- keep us. Just as a sailor who keeps his ship is kept by the ship, so His word keeps those who accept it. To accept His word means to experience

His spiritual presence and joy. He manifests Himself in the life of those by whom His word is accepted.

It is love for Him that prompts acceptance of His word. Love is a deliberate principle of the mind. It is a purposeful achievement of the will. It is a victory over natural temperament. His love within enables one to resolve, "No matter what a person does to me, I will always seek His highest good." Those who love have a mental awareness prompting a consciousness that no matter what a person is like, God seeks nothing but his highest good. So must we who serve in His name.

Jesus appealed for acceptance of His word on the basis it was validated by His work. "Believe me," He said, "for the sake of the works themselves" (John 14: 11). His works are still looked upon skeptically by some. Could He have performed miracles? Hume, Spinosa, and other modern cynics answer with a resounding, "No: logic and experience say they were impossible." Whose logic and experience?

Marco Polo returned from his visit to the land of the Khans with tales of the splendor of their empire. His native Venetians had never heard of such things as he related much less had seen them. He was accused of lying. Even upon his deathbed priests appealed to him to repent and renounce his fantasy. Though the experience of Europeans did not at that time validate his account to be true, his logic and experience sustained him.

We who did not live when Christ performed His miracles do not have reason to accept them based on our logic and circumstances. However, those who were alive at the time and saw them confirmed them as their observations. Skeptics refuse to accept what contradicts their experience. An Eskimo returning from Hawaii might have difficulty convincing his friends as to what a pineapple is. Their adventure would not logically confirm the existence of this tropical fruit. Any anti-miracle mentality is an attempt to dethrone God in favor of individual experience. Records of eye witnesses confirm for us that which we have not personally observed. We can accept His works by the same reasoning we accept Hannibal crossing the Alps using elephants. The records regarding Christ's miracles are far more complete and numerous. A miracle, after all, is only a miracle from our perspective. For God it is all in a day's work.

Genesis contains the thrilling account of creation. Included, it seems almost as a parenthetical expression, a statement showing the Creator's capacity. As the writer is moving away from the story, he adds as though an after-thought, "He made the stars also" (Genesis 1: 16). Like a person walking away and looking back over the shoulder the writer seems to say, "Oh, yes, by the way, as a part of His creation package, He decided to throw in the stars." Consider the stars, rather one little collection, one of our nearest neighbors, the Andromeda Galaxy. It contains over 200 billion suns larger than our one. A light year is 6 trillion miles, the distance traveled in a year moving at the speed of light. Andromeda is over 2 million light years from our Milky Way. Our fastest space craft, Voyager II, would require 150 billion years to reach Andromeda. This vastness can be multiplied by many other galaxies.

"He made the stars also." How many? No one knows, but it is estimated that if you had started counting them on the day Christ was born and counted them at the rate of one a second you would not be half through counting. It was all in a day's work for the Creator.

I believe all these startling facts. I do not believe them because my experience verifies them or logic suggests them. I accept them by faith. Every day each of us accepts hundreds of things equally unverifiable by our own experience.

Luke 1:49 says, "He who is mighty has done great things for me; and holy is his name." Three days after Jesus completed His demonstration and teaching session in the upper room, He was to do "the great thing," and by it His holy name would be verified. His resurrection was to verify His works. It was the Father's way of substantiating, authenticating, and validating the words of the Son. Christ's life and all He taught was acceptable to the Lord God Jehovah. If He accepted the works and words of the Suffering Servant, so can we. As His servants, we must "keep" His word. This means we are to - - -

TO OBEY

Enfolded in the teaching of the New Testament is a repetitious theme. As the Apostle Paul pressed westward across Achaia, Macedonia, Galatia, and eventually Rome, he stressed the theme of "obedience to the faith". For him faith was far more than intellectual assent or even admirable trust; it was a life style of obedience. As two sides of one sandwich, he presented to them "trust and obey" as an essential element in the diet of all who professed to follow Christ.

George Washington, in issuing a presidential proclamation in 1789 related to the holiday of Thanksgiving, evidenced an awareness of the need for obedience. It stated in part:

> "Whereas it is the duty of all nations to acknowledge the providence of Almighty God, to obey His will, to be grateful for His benefits, and humbly implore His protection and favor..."

Obedience to the words of Christ is not imposed upon us by force, but faith makes it incumbent upon us.

The Greek word for "obey" is HUPAKOUO. The simple root verb, AKOUO, means "to hear". The prefixed preposition, HUPA, means "under". Thus, the word means to hear under authority. Gradually the word grew to mean to submit to the authority of the one heard, to obey. A servant is under the authority of his master. What he hears from his master, his authority, he is to submit to. When the Christian community develops this mentality a revolution will occur. It will be a revolution of obedient service to the Lord.

Our society seems to have an ambition to reserve and preserve itself into perpetual life on this planet. This is antithetical to the teachings of Christ which call for self-sacrificing service in obedience to His commandments.

Charlemagne, "Emperor of the Romans" from 800 to 814, was a key figure in development of western Europe's medieval civilization. The "empire" he revived lasted for nearly a thousand years. Culturally and politically he left such a mark on the newly rising civilization of the West that biographers say no ruler of the Middle Ages more deserved the title of "The Great." He was buried in Aux-la-chapel in France. His body was placed in his marble coronation chair sitting upright. He was dressed in his imperial robes. In his left hand was his scepter, on his head was his jeweled crown. His right hand rested on a Bible open on his lap.

Many years later when the burial chamber was opened the robes had virtually turned to dust. The crown had fallen on the floor and the scepter had slipped from his hand. The skeletal index finger of his right hand rested on the Bible pointing to the text which reads: "What is a man profited, if he shall gain the whole world, and lose his own soul?"

Someday our molded, physical remains will be all that evidences our former presence on this planet. Then faithful obedient service to the words of our Lord will have just begun to pay dividends in Heaven. Not only does obedience to His word gain rewards in Heaven, it gives renewal in time.

Charles I, grandson of Charlemagne, had a daughter, Princess Elizabeth. A marble monument erected by Queen Victoria marks her burial location in Newport Church on the Isle of Wight. Though accustomed to an opulent lifestyle, she was imprisoned in Carisbrook Castle during the time of her father's difficulties. As a princess she lived to serve the King of Kings even during her imprisonment. Separated from her friends and family, she lived a lonely existence in her sorrowful cell until death relieved her. Her lifeless body was found in her bed with her Bible open before her and her finger resting on the text which read: "Come unto Me, all ye that labor, and are heaven laden, and I will give you rest". Newport's monument to her memory confirms this with the inscription: "Riches and rank cannot make you happy. Jesus only can satisfy the soul."

Obedience and happiness feed on each other. Obedience nurses happiness and happiness nourishes obedience. Those who border on obedience are of all people most miserable. Acts of disobedience make them discontent. Acts of obedience are so infrequent as to make them dissatisfied apart from full obedience. It is full obedience to Christ's word that satisfies.

Speaking of the will and words of the Lord the Psalmist says, "...in keeping of them there is great reward" (Psalms 19:11). This does not speak of deferred payment. He said "in" keeping them "is" great reward. Inherent in obedience is a part of the reward. Obedience and reward are coexistent.

In Psalms 19: 7 - 11 eight insights are revealed regarding "keeping" the "commandment of the Lord."

* It is PERFECT - "The law of the Lord is perfect" (Verse 7). It is considered "perfect" because it is complete, nothing needs to be added. It is correct, nothing needs to be changed. It is clean, nothing needs to be taken out. It is consistent, nothing needs to be conditioned upon extraneous sources.

* It is PRODUCTIVE - "converting the soul" (Verse 7). By His word He changes persons from disobedient rebels to obedient servants, from darkness to light, and

from death to life. By "keeping" His word this miraculous change is achieved. The word "converting" should not be limited to anything short of a saving change of heart. The word translated "converting" is the same word for "restoring". Thus, obedient servants can have their vitality restored by reading and complying with His word.

* It is PLAIN - "making wise the simple" (Verse 7). Even a person not endowed with great mental capacity and/or deprived of formal education can act wisely by obeying His word. Enough of it is complex enough to confound the wise. Likewise, enough of it is elemental enough to inform and inspire a child. God doesn't send mixed signals. The challenge is not in understanding it, but obeying it. This word is said to be "sure". In Hebrew the word is a participle of the verb, from which the adverb "amen" is derived. It means there is no doubt about a statement once God has made it. It can be believed.

* It is PLEASING - "rejoicing the heart" (Verse 8). A classic con game has been played in making God's way seem unpleasant and unprofitable. An inversion of values has resulted in His word seeming harsh and hard. Satan has achieved this because, as opposed to God who loves you, he hates you. Joy is inherent in doing God's will. Any moment of disobedience robs a person of that time being filled with joy.

* It is PURE - "the commandment of the Lord is pure" (Verse 8). The Lord is holy; therefore, anything issuing from Him must of necessity be pure. No contaminants can be found in His word. The Creator of the universe, which at its inception was perfect, would have no difficulty creating a book. A perfect God would have no difficulty providing a perfect book. His word is without mixture of motive or content. It is unadulterated and undiluted. The

traditions of man are fallacious and fallible. The text of God's word is tried and true. Nevertheless, our opinion of it is not as important as our obedience to it.

* It is PERMANENT - "enduring forever" (Verse 9). This does not merely speak of durability but, also, of applicability. It is His dateless and ageless norm for all ages. Those who argue that everything is relative forget His word is instead relevant to everything. In the field of physics, there is an axiom: "For every action there is an equal and opposite reaction." In the field of chemistry, there is a truth: "Every formula must balance." These are not variables. They have always been true and shall always be factual. In the spiritual world, the word of the Lord changes not. It is always germane.

From the dawning of creation no new laws of nature have been given. They are constant. This principle is true of God's word also. It is constant. The word of the Lord is a transcript of the character of God.

Books by human authors have their day and fade. Few are long lasting on the "Best Seller" list. Many major libraries are mere cemeteries for dead books. Some have a productive past, but being dated, have passed their day of honor.

* It is PRICELESS -- "More to be desired...than gold" (Verse 10). The value of God's word to the human race is of inestimable value. A world devoid of it would be a world of spiritual anarchy and physical chaos. Those instances where it has not been obeyed verify this. This is true of individual lives and national governments. The value of gold is established. Years ago Cherokee Indians stole seven fifty pound bars of gold from the U.S. Government near the mint at Dahlonega, Georgia. This gold has never been found. Today, if valued at $700 an ounce, it would be worth

$3,920,000. Of even greater value is the priceless word of God. Gold can only give value, but the word of God gives meaning to life.

* It is PROTECTIVE - "by them is thy servant warned" (Verse 11). His precepts are intended to prevent Him grief and us guilt. His warnings are intended to help us avoid those attitudes and actions not good for us. He never asks to do one thing for any reason other than our good. He never asks us not to do one thing except for our good. God has our welfare in mind in every chapter of His word. Some accuse Him of using scare tactics to manipulate people. A sailor posted on the bow of a ship who sees a mine in the direct course of the ship is not using scare tactics when he informs the commanding officer. Even though the warning might scare the crew, the action is not intended to frighten. Forewarning and sparing the crew is the motive. So it is with God's word. Adherence to it can prevent much misery for His servant.

The concept of being "warned" carries the idea of being instructed in that which is good as well as advised against that which is wrong. Negatively applied it is preventive. Positively applied it is productive.

TO STAND GUARD OVER

Repetitiously, in His last hours with the disciples, Christ spoke of the responsibility to "keep" His words. It was optimum test of love. One of the three principle applications of the word "keep" means to "stand guard over". He was in effect saying, "I am entrusting the preservation and perpetuation of my word and works to your guardianship."Faithfulness was exercised in originating the Bible as His word. Dr. JohnR. Sampey, former President of Southern Baptist Seminary in Louisville, Kentucky, remarked, "The Holy Spirit was too good a guard of the inspiration of Scripture to have allowed an error in it in part or in whole." It is in whole the "pure" word of a holy God. The Lord has entrusted for safe "keep" His inspired word. None of it came by "private interpretation" (II Peter 1: 20). This statement referred to its origin. Neither does it consist of "cunningly devised fables" (II Peter 1: 16). It was the product of "holy men of God" being "moved by the Holy Spirit" (II Peter 1:21). The Holy Spirit stood guard over it as it was penned. Faithful servants obeyed revelation given them by the Spirit and willingly wrote in their words the Word of God. Their stewardship was that of scribes.

* Augustine said, "To the canonical Scriptures alone I owe agreement without dissent". Such was his pledge of allegiance.

* Oswald Chambers faithfully warned, "Beware of reasoning about God's Word -- obey it!"

* Martin Luther revealed his reason for a resolute will by commenting, "My conscience is captive to the Word of God".

* J.I. Packer recorded his opinion by noting, "To defer to God's Word is an act of faith; any querying and editing of it on our own initiative is an exhibition of unbelief."

*   John Wesley, out of a revived heart wrote, "I am a Bible
        bigot. I follow it in all things, both great and small".

*   Thomas Watson recorded his mind on the matter by
        observing, "Had I the tongue of angels, I could not
        sufficiently set forth the excellency of Scripture".

PRESERVATION is an important part of standing guard over the word.

Jude found it expedient to write an epistle on the urgency of contending for the faith (Jude 3). The word "faith" is used here of the thing believed not the act of believing. It is a reference to the body of doctrine contained in the totality of Scripture. Servants of the Lord have been made custodians of the oracles of God. It, having been delivered to His servants, is to be defended by them. All who profess to follow Him must unashamedly vie for the bequest given.

Anytime there is an original of value counterfeits follow. Rolex watches, Gucci bags, Louis Vuitton luggage, Chanel No. 5 perfume, and U.S. Government $20.00 bills are all counterfeited because of their worth. Satan, the original deceiver, deals only in the fraudulent. He has authored spurious scripture, phony precepts, erroneous interpretations, deceitful discipleship and cunning commentary. Why? He has done so simply because he realizes what many who profess to follow Christ have failed to understand. Christ's word is essential to eternal life including its consummation, confirmation and culmination.

Paul sought to impress on young Timothy, and all of us blessed to read the first letter received by him, the importance of guarding the Word: "O Timothy! Guard what was committed to your trust, avoiding the vain babbling and contradictions of what is falsely called knowledge --- by professing it, some have strayed concerning the faith" (I Timothy 6: 20, 21).

John, known for his love, stressed the imperative importance of keeping the word: "Whoever keeps His word, truly the word of God is perfected in him" (I John 2: 5). He further emphasized the blessing of keeping the word: "For this is the love of God, that we keep his commandments: and His commandments are not burdensome" (I John 5:3).

From the isolation of Patmos, John wrote the prophetic book which concludes the New Testament, the Revelation. Therein he stated:

"Blessed is he w h o reads, and those who hear the words of this prophecy, and keep those things which are written in it..." (Revelation 1: 3).

Every servant should seek to avoid being contentious while contending for the faith. This calls for no compromise of conviction or consorting with compromisers. It necessitates that the contesting be done in a spirit of Christ like love. Love for the commandments of Christ motivates sympathetic love for those who don't know any better than to distort it.

PERPETUATION is an important part of standing guard over the word.

It is estimated that 40 percent of the American population has no Christian memory. That is, four out of every ten Americans have no background involving any Christian teaching or experience. They are ignorant of scripture. If the Word is to be perpetuated, it must be propagated. An influx of people from foreign countries accounts for much of this lack of experiential Christian heritage. A critical cause of some is parental presumption. Many adults assume their children have their same set of values. Because the parents had a youthful orientation in Christian culture, they falsely conclude their children have their awareness of Bible truth. Frequently, the children have no personal experience in the church or familiarity with the Scripture. They are Biblically illiterate. Christ's servants in obedience to His command are to evangelize and disciple persons. Failure in this assignment is producing a pagan society on a foundation of Christian ancestry.

Cultivation by example often has to precede actual direct evangelization. One is more likely to hear a witness from a person who has performed a service for them than from an unrelated person.

Dionysius, a pagan scholar who became a Christian and later Bishop of Alexandria from A.D. 247 to A.D. 269 wrote of the involvement of Christians during a plague. "Most of our brethren did not spare themselves and held together in the closest love of their neighbors. They were not afraid to visit the sick, to look after them and to take care of them for Christ's sake, and to die joyfully with them. But the heathen did exactly the opposite. They cast out any who began to be sick, deserted those who were dearest to them, threw the sick and half-dead into the streets, and left the dead unburied."

Later one commentator wrote of the word's of Dionysius: "When the life of the Christian group is recognizably different from the life of the world outside, then no tricks are needed to attract people".

The bishop merely observed his people obeying the commandments of Christ in a manner becoming of one assigned to stand guard over them; to keep them. Those who keep His Word are recognizably different. It is this difference that attracts others to the One who makes such a difference in a life. Vitality still resides in this verse by Edgar A. Guest.

"I'd rather see a sermon than hear one any day.

I'd rather one would walk with me than merely point the way.

Fine counsel is confusing, but example is always clear.

The eye is a better pupil, and more discerning than the ear.

Fine counsel is confusing but example is always clear."

The world is yet to find a successful argument against the changed life of an obedient servant of Christ. Set your mind upon the role of a servant and let nothing deter or defer you from serving in His beloved name.

As the events of the upper room were about to end, Christ concluded, "But that the world may know that I love the Father; and as the Father gave me commandment, so I do. Arise, let us go from here" (John 14:31). Christ was about to obey the commandment of the Father in such a way as to have every right to expect His followers to accept by faith, obey, and stand guard over His commandments.

He left the room to become obedient even unto death. That is the price servants sometimes have to pay. Anything less is a down payment of faithfulness. Jesus left the upper room fully conscious of what awaited. It would have been impossible to live in that land and not be familiar with crucifixion. Brutality as invented by the Romans was common knowledge. How then could He calmly go forth willingly to face His hour of agony?

Jesus had a mind set, a purpose. Earlier He had said of the events soon to follow: "...for this purpose I came to this hour" (John 12: 27). Later, before Pilate, He reiterated this, "For this cause was I born, and for this cause I have come into the world, that I should bear witness to the truth" (John 18: 37).

A significant summary of His life's purpose was recorded from His lips by Matthew: "Just as the Son of Man did not come to be served, but to serve, and to give His life a ransom for many" (Matthew 20:28). His mind was set on the fact that He did not come to be served, but to serve. Only by simulation of his Master can a servant be fulfilled. "The servant is not greater than his master" (John 13: 16).

Jesus' example as a servant must not only be admired, but emulated. We are to serve as He. This service must be consistent and always contemporary. Don't let isolated memories of sporadic service sit like old men on the park bench of your mind.

Those who serve Christ can only do so consistently if they have a mind-set and interpret the things that happen to them as opportunities to serve. By having a mind-set of a servant, things that might normally be interpreted as obstacles can be viewed as opportunities; adversities become advantages. Here is the ultimate test to determine if you have the mind-set of a servant. Observe how you react the next time somebody treats you like a servant. A second screening of your spirit of servitude relates to your speech. Anybody can talk the talk. However, suppose you suddenly became a mute. Without your words could people tell you are a servant of the Lord by your actions alone? Suppose your actions of the last month were on video tape without a voice track. By viewing your actions, would persons be able to tell you have a servant temperament?

Another way to x-ray your attitude toward service would involve your neighbors. If they were asked to name five things that characterize you, would one of them be a spirit of servanthood?

Shortly before Jesus and His disciples went to Jerusalem for this last time that "He steadfastly set His face to go to Jerusalem" (Luke 9: 51). This was a contemporary Semitic idiom meaning He resolutely made up His mind to go to the designated place of His passion. His mind was fully made up. High resolve and deep love made His face fixed and His footsteps firm. This was the ultimate sublime, whole-hearted devotion of a faithful servant. "Let this mind be in you, which was also in Christ Jesus" (Philippians 2: 5).

CHAPTER 7

THE MISSION OF A SERVANT

The Mount of Olives was second only to the Sea of Galilee as a favorite retreat spot for Jesus and His disciples. Compassionately He had viewed the Golden City of Jerusalem from here and wept. His gaze focused on the 1,000 square foot temple plateau on the summit of Mt. Zion. Some stones used to construct the temple were 20 by 40 feet and weighed 100 tons. Pillars supporting Solomon's Porch were 37 feet high and of such circumference that three men could not reach around them. An ornate bridge from the lower city to the upper spanned the Tyropoeon Valley. This is what He saw, but what He beheld was the need of the people.

Soon He would depart Jerusalem for the final time, cross the Brook Kidron, and enter the beautiful Garden of Gethsemane at the base of the Mount of Olives. That walk was but a few hundred yards. When He would last cross the brook it would be Passover night, a full moon. By the light of the moon, He would be able to see clearly the brook flowing with the blood of over 200,000 lambs slain in the Temple in preparation for Passover. Soon their prophetic role would be fulfilled in the shedding of His own blood as the Suffering Servant.

Gethsemane, the place of an olive press, would accommodate His final private hour of agony. There for the last time He would weep not only over Jerusalem, but the sin of the world.

His present moment of retreat to Olivet followed a teaching visit in the Temple. His speech there had evoked questions among His disciples. Privately the twelve came to Him and asked three questions. His responses, known as the "Olivet Discourse" have challenged scholars for generations. They asked:

"When shall these things be?" referring to the destruction of the temple.

"What shall be the sign of your coming?"

"What shall be the sign ... of the end of the world?"

One of the questions related to His second coming. Still a bit foggy minded about Who He was and what His mission was the twelve had no comprehension of what He spoke. By the Holy Spirit aiding Matthew's recall, Christ's great revelation was remembered and recorded. Set like a rare gem in His address is a strategic statement related to servanthood. These remarks came at the time Christ's popularity with the masses was at its height. Only days earlier His followers had thrilled over the mass of persons in Jerusalem for the Passover cheering His entrance into the city. "Hosanna! Blessed is He who comes in the name of the Lord" (John 12: 13) had filled their minds as it had the air. A massive tide of momentum had swung in favor of Jesus.

No modern rock star has ever entered a stage to greater acclaim. At this moment He was a celebrated celebrity. Mystics and militants, the local populace and loyal pilgrims wanted Him to assert His leadership. Only the hard core pious religious leaders were fearful of Him.

One home owner had given Him his upper room in which to celebrate Passover, large crowds had gathered at the homes of Zacchaeus in Jericho and Lazarus in Bethany to see Him, a wealthy resident of Jerusalem had afforded Him his valued donkey, persons had torn down palm branches to line the streets which they had blanketed with their robes. Jerusalem was His. It is little wonder that His entrance is still called "The Triumphant Entry."

That grand day was a fulfillment of prophecy. Daniel had stated the time (Daniel 9: 24 - 26). A careful calculation reveals it was to be 173,880 days after being foretold. Passover was always celebrated on the 15th of Nisan, mid-April. Jesus came to Bethany six days before Passover and entered Jerusalem the next day, April 6, 32 A.D. That was precisely 173,880 days after the prophecy of Daniel. Thus, the Father had further validated the Son as Messiah.

Here again Jesus humbled Himself. Reverie now replaces revelry. Seated on the Mount of Olives He had a full view of the walled city of Jerusalem in all of its splendor. Historian Josephus wrote of Jerusalem: "The outward face of the temple in its front wanted nothing that was likely to surprise either men's minds or their eyes; for it was covered all over with plates of gold of great weight, and, at the first rising of the sun, reflected back a very fiery splendor, and made those who forced themselves to look upon it to turn away their eyes, just as they would have done at the sun's own rays."

A close look at the eyes of the Lord as He sat looking at Jerusalem revealed they were not dazzled, but tearful. He saw not the splendor of the edifices. Instead He was conscious of the condition of the people therein. The word that tells of His being moved with compassion is the root for our word seismograph. He was visibly shaken.

His spirit, not the shouts of the crowd, influenced what He was about to say. Once again His subject was to be servanthood. His disciples must have thought, "Not now Jesus, not here. This is your moment to bask in glory." Knowing His exodus, about which He spoke with Moses and Elijah on the Mount of Transfiguration, to be at hand, He chose once more to speak about servanthood. He embodied it in a narrative to illustrate the importance of obedience even in His absence. Hear Him tell the story:

"Watch therefore, for you do not know what hour your Lord is coming. But know this, that if the master of the house had known what hour the thief would come, he would have watched, and not allowed his house to be broken into. Therefore, you also be ready: for the Son of Man is coming at an hour when you do not expect Him. Who then is a faithful and wise servant, whom his master made ruler over his household, to give them food in due season? Blessed is that servant, whom his master, when he comes, will find so doing. Assuredly, I say to you that He will make him ruler over all his goods" (Matthew 24: 42 - 47).

Summarized: "That servant who does what his lord wants him to do when it should be done will be fulfilled, happy, and honored." From that it can be concluded that abundant life results from finding God's will and doing it. That is not the world's philosophy. However, it is strange that those of the world who speak and write of happiness are often those who have experienced the least.

AN EXPLANATION OF OBEDIENCE TO AUTHORITY

What Christ was about to do would later be described by Paul in these words: "...he humbled himself, and became obedient unto death..." (Philippians 2: 8). A primary characteristic of a servant is that he is under authority. Ownership is the issue. Obedience issues from ownership. Prior to departure from heaven it was agreed that Jesus would relinquish His supernatural power in so far as using it for Himself. Therefore, on earth He never once used it for His advantage, only for the welfare of others. Personally He operated as any individual with an independent free will. He had relinquished His authority to the Father. Only after His resurrection would He say, "all authority has been given, to me in heaven and on earth" (Matthew 28: 18).

In each moment of decision Jesus was free to choose to be obedient or disobedient. Being in all ways tempted just as we, He could have at any moment violated the will of the Father. When confronting temptation He was not play acting, pretending to be tempted. If that were true, His whole mission on earth would have been a charade.

The degree of His obedience can be easily measured. Old Testament prophecy relating to Him was His pre-written biography. Numerous prophecies told of what He would be and do. Once on His earthly mission, He was free to choose to do, or not to do, what was said of Him. At issue was whether He would be faithfully obedient under the authority of God's word.

As an example Isaiah the prophet spoke of aspects of His mission: "The Spirit of the Lord God is upon me; because the Lord has anointed me to preach good tidings to the poor; He hath sent Me to heal the brokenhearted, to proclaim liberty to the captives, and the opening of the prison to them that are bound; To proclaim the acceptable year of the Lord, and the day of vengeance of our God; to comfort all that mourn ..." (Isaiah 61: 1,2). In retrospect it was written of Him: "Behold, I come --- In the volume of the book it is written of Me --- to do your will, O God..." (Hebrews 10: 7 & 9).

Not only was the Old Testament His Bible, it was His biography written in advance. For Him to accomplish His mission His life must be the lake of fulfillment into which ALL the rivers of prophecy flow. At any moment He could have disobeyed the authority of God's Word.

All authority is rooted in God Himself. He has established a norm for us as He did for Jesus. Our standard of authority, like that of Jesus, is the scripture. As the Word of God, it is the highest authority on earth. The authenticity and general integrity of the New Testament make its teachings as binding upon us as the Old Testament prophecies regarding Messiah were on Christ.

Billy Graham said, "I am convinced that people are open to the Christian message if it is seasoned with authority and proclaimed as God's own Word." For years people responded to the invitation of this faithful evangelist offered against the background of his often repeated statement, "The Bible says..." He offers no higher authority.

Of more importance that what you parrot as your belief about the Bible is do you obey it?

In Reno, Nevada, I heard a partially-educated individual who had great faith comment on the Bible. He was asked if he believed in the verbal inspiration of Scripture. He replied, "I sure do. I believe in the verbal inspiration, the adverbial inspiration, the nounal and pronounal inspiration, and the conjunctional inspiration of the Bible." That beautiful kind of confidence in Scriptural authority must be complimented by obedience to its teachings.

It is self-evident how disastrous it would have been to Jesus' mission if He had not submitted to the authority of God's Word. It is no less frustrating to God's purpose for our life when we disobey Biblical instruction given us.

God's Word was denigrated and neutralized by traditions when Jesus came. Presently, instead of going to God's Word to see what it says other sources are sought by many. Even when pushed by the wise men at the time of Christ's birth the scribes had to search the Scripture to find where He was to be born. Upon finding when and where, they did not get up off their apathy and travel those ten short miles to Bethlehem to see Him. To them reading God's Word was a religious exercise. Acceptance of its authority was an act of intellectual conformity not supported by submission to its authority.

All that anyone can know with assurance concerning God comes from the Bible alone. It is the only and ultimate authority. His authority rests in it not the priesthood, a creed, a church, or an experience. This concept does not make the Bible a god and therefore subject mankind to the charge of worshipping the book or Bibliolatry. Rather, it holds that the bible is God's recorded revelation; a sure source of knowledge concerning God, His will, word, and work. It, being God's Word, it has its authority in its Author.

There is an insidious denial of biblical authority. It is disobedience to its teaching. If Scripture truly is God's inerrant Word, it demands our full attention and loving obedience. Refusal to obey the Bible is as dangerous as embracing certain critical methods that seek to refute biblical inerrancy. To live in a way that conflicts with the Bible's teaching discredits its authority as absolutely as questioning its credibility or endorsing the documentary hypothesis. One is disobedience in theory and the other in practice. They are equal errors.

Dr. R.G. Lee, faithful pastor of Bellevue Baptist Church for years, was a man with uninhibited confidence in the creditability of Scripture. His devout life was lived in obedience to it. Of the Scripture he said: "The Bible, inerrant in statement, infallible in authority, immeasurable in influence, inexhaustive in its adequacy, personal in application, regenerative in power, inspired in totality, is the miracle Book of diversity in unity, of harmony in infinite complexity --

the God- breathed Book that travels more highways, walks more bypaths, knocks at more doors, and speaks to more people in their mother tongue than any other book the world has ever known, can ever know, will ever know."

A person may profess to believe as he, but consistent disobedience is a total disclaimer. Profession and practice must be congruent. Obedience alone authenticates authority.

AN EXHORTATION TO OBEDIENCE TO AUTHORITY

We now live in the period spoken of by Jesus in His narrative between the lord's going away and coming again. All that the servant had to go on in the absence of his lord was the word of his lord. Authority rested in the lord himself before his departure and returned to him upon his return. In the interim his word was the authority. His word was his verbalized will made known. Obedience to the word was obedience to the lord. Martin Luther lived in a day when the authority of God's Word had been superceded by papal authority. Knowing that no priesthood of believers was to interpret the Bible according to their whims, but all were obligated to obey it in its fullest he wrote:

"If I profess with the loudest voice and clearest exposition every portion of the truth of God except precisely that little point which the world and the devil are at that moment attacking, I am not confessing Christ, however boldly I may be professing Christ. Where the battle rages there the loyalty of the soldier is proved and to be steady on all the battlefront besides is mere flight and disgrace if he flinches at that point". Today "that point" is Scriptural authority in theological circles and personal lives. Holding a strong view of Scripture and not holding to it is contradictory.

A moment of decision charts our course. Standing on the beautiful Bernina Pass in Switzerland, the enchanting Engadine is on one side and on the other the vast expanse of Italy. Nearby are two small lakes separated by only a narrow watershed. Though close in their points of origin, the water from one flows into the Adriatic Sea and that from the other into the Black Sea. Every person has his own Bernina Pass, a time when the flow of the course of life is determined. A choice to obey is a choice favoring a fulfilled life.

With that understanding engage in this practical activity. Check yourself regarding obedience to our Lord's Word in these areas:

Have you presented your body to the Lord as a living sacrifice (Romans 12:1), or are you continuing to walk according to the flesh (Romans 8: 5 - 7) as if you still do not belong to your Lord?

Do you think of yourself more highly than you ought (Romans 12: 3) and allow fits of hypocrisy to pervert the love you profess (Romans 12: 9)?

Is your loyalty divided between God and mammon (Matthew 6: 24)?

Are you neglecting your prayer life (Luke 18: 1, 2) and Bible study (II Timothy 2: 15)?

Are you living in a state of anxiety or discontent (Philippians 4: 6, 11)?

Do you by exercising malice and envy stir up strife (Romans 13: 13)?

Are you fulfilling your role as an ambassador (II Corinthians 5: 19, 20) and witness (Matthew 28: 19, 20)?

Are you seeking first the kingdom, the rule of God, in your life (Matthew 6: 33)?

In fulfillment of the authoritative command to "seek first" the kingdom do you:

Give God the first part of the first hour of the day?

Give Him the first day of the week for public worship? Give Him a tithe as the first fruit of your labor?

Give Him first place in decision making?

Give Him the position of Lord in your home and work?

If not what use is there in professing belief in the authority of God's Word? Failure to study God's Word is a common act of disobedience. It is ludicrous to profess to believe the Bible and not know its content. Only by reading and studying can it be known. It can't be absorbed by osmosis. Professed ignorance of a command is no excuse for not executing it.

Suppose a U.S. Ambassador to a foreign country received a letter from the president. Contained in the letter are specific instructions regarding an action to be taken by the ambassador at once. Days laps and no news of compliance is received by the president. A courier is dispatched who enquires of the ambassador regarding his receipt of the letter. Being assured the letter was received, the courier probes further regarding compliance with the order of the president. Lack of compliance has already discredited the president in certain quarters. Failure to execute has given the people of the land in which the ambassador served a wrong impression. "Why did you disobey the orders of the president?" the courier asks. Apologetically the ambassador answers, "I didn't know the orders." Puzzled the courier probes, "Didn't know the orders? Didn't you receive the letter?" Hesitatingly response is given, "Yes, but I haven't opened it yet. I am sure the president will understand that I didn't do his bidding simply because I didn't know it." In follow-up the president doesn't understand. Failure to receive an order is in itself an act of disobedience to authority. The ambassador is recalled and replaced with an obedient and responsible one.

Our failure to read the Bible, that is, to receive the orders is in itself an act of disobedience.

Daily a believer's mind is bombarded with precepts and principles contrary to the Word of God. Every form of media programs the mind with secular thought. Public systems of education teach as though there is no God. Entertainment is void of anything supportive of Christian character. The mind swims in a sea of secular humanism. A regimented program of Bible study is needed to counteract this negativism.

Albert Einstein said, "One incorrect input requires eleven correct inputs to correct." By that he meant that five minutes of negative programming requires fifty-five minutes of positive programming to correct. With no daily Bible input there is no correction and disobedience is inevitable.

The Law of Emotional Gravity dominates a life without an orientation of Biblical obedience. Simply states it is: "one pessimist can pull five optimists down easier than five optimists can lift up one pessimist." Only by association with people of the Book and personal submissive study of it can a person compensate for this inviolable law.

In telling His story, Jesus said the servant most blessed is the one found "doing" by his lord upon his return. Service is the sign of a servant. To obey is better than sacrifice. We are to be doers of the Word and not debaters only.

AN EXPECTATION OF OBEDIENCE TO AUTHORITY

On the Mount of Olives that day Jesus made it plain that faithful servants were honored and rewarded. He was no less clear regarding the punishment given those garnering the displeasure of their lord because of disobedience. Note His insight into treatment given the unfaithful servant: "The master of that servant will come on a day when he is not looking for him, and at an hour that he is not aware of, and shall cut him into and appoint him his portion with the hypocrites. There shall be weeping and gnashing of teeth" (Matthew 24: 50, 51). Before considering punishment inflicted, it must be noted that Jesus was merely stating the custom of the day. Secondly, it must be observed that this was not a true servant, but instead an imposter posing deceptively for a time.

The unfaithful servant, the pretender, was "dichotomized," that is, cut in pieces. Such servants were cut up or cut into with a horrible saw because of disobedience (II Samuel 12: 31; I Chronicles 20: 3). He has "his portion with the hypocrites" because he being one of them was a counterfeit servant.

A master had the right to do with a servant as he pleased. In telling this story, Jesus is reminding us that a servant had no rights of his own. The issue was ownership. By our standards the idea of legally being able to cut a person in two and not being punished for it is abhorrent. Jesus was not endorsing the act. The point is that by noting this custom Jesus was once more calling attention to the fact that a servant had no rights of his own. His rights rest with his master. Servants were preoccupied with their responsibilities not their rights. Three characteristics of this fraud were made evident by Christ.

He was presumptuous. He thought he could deceive his master who would not be back for a long time. Delayed accountability gave energy to disobedience.

He was peremptory. Acting coercively he abused others. Arrogance caused him haughtily to impose on others. His dominant will was sadistically imposed.

He was profligate. He indulged himself by over eating and being drunk. Dissipation typifies disobedience.

Evidently none of these traits had been shown in the presence of his lord. This two-faced conduct was the reason he was classified with the hypocrites and received their punishment. Contrast between unfaithfulness and faithfulness was shown by function. One was obedient and the other disobedient. The obedient servant was rewarded and the disobedient one punished along with his co-hypocrites.

Rejection of authority is shown in failure in duty and reliability is revealed by fidelity in duty.

After His crucifixion and before His final ascension our Lord appeared to His disciples and said, "Behold my hands and my feet, that it is I myself. Handle Me, and see, for a spirit does not have flesh and bones, as you see I have" (Luke 24: 39).

Our Lord, like the lord in His story, has gone away into the distant land of heaven. He is coming again. We live in the parenthesis of time between His two advents. We rejoice to know He is with us and will be always. However, He has no hands and feet to be touched and with which to touch. A spirit does not have.

Upon His departure Jesus appointed the Holy Spirit to be His invisible presence with us. He has "no flesh and bones" in a world "flesh and bones" oriented. For that reason "God hath sent forth the Spirit of his Son into your hearts" (Galatians 4: 6). His Spirit has no flesh and bones other than that of believers.

He has none but yours if you are a Christian. This forms a unique relationship. It is God in you. This is the only remaining hope of glory. Only as we obediently fulfill our roles does the world have a demonstration of a servant. In considering that role, remember it is enough for a servant to be like his master. Christ is the role model we are to pattern for the world. This can be done with confidence. Our Lord's last earthly step was taken on the Mount of Olives. Just before His bodily ascension He said, "All power is given unto me in heaven and in earth" (Matthew 28: 18).

Excitement ripples through the Christian world at that very thought. We think of His energizing and enabling power available to surge through His obedient servant. Courage and comfort is gained from that stimulating thought. "He who is in you is greater than he who is in the world" (I John 4:4). Holy boldness is derived from knowing that in our confrontation with evil we have an indwelling greater power. Nothing should be allowed to diminish that fact.

However, in our Lord's farewell statement a different word is used than that which means ability. There are two Greek words often translated "power". One speaks of ability. The other means authority. We often become so preoccupied with our Lord's ability and our desire for Him to exercise it for our good that we forget about His authority over us.

In stating His "Magna Carta" on Olivet for His soon to emerge church, He promised to be with His followers: "I am with you always, even to the end of the age" (Matthew 28: 20). By this we are reassured of His ability. In reality He wasn't on that occasion speaking of His ability to aid us, but His presence with us for the purpose of exercising authority over us. His presence is not just for our comfort but for His control.

Our mission on earth is to occupy under His authority until He comes. We are to serve Him by fulfilling our assigned tasks. Our obedience to His will should be no less than if He were our personal companion. His bodily absence does not lessen our accountability. His return is imminent and our report is inevitable.

It is imperative that we be consistent and tenacious. One of the bitterest memories of World War I was the battle at Gallipoli. A brave contingency battled its way ashore where the Dardanelles and the Aegean Sea meet. Courageously they fought their way almost to Constantinople. The Turks who occupied the city gave up hope. They were out of food and down to their last rounds of ammunition. Supposing themselves to be defeated, they prepared the order for the evacuation of Constantinople. The allied force not being aware of the plight of their opponent suddenly disengaged and withdrew. Though near to victory their disobedience cost them the victory. There is a spiritual lesson to be learned from that page of history. A servant must never -- never, waver or retreat. The plight of the opposition matters not. It is our pledge to our commander that is of consequence.

Would the physical presence of Christ motivate you any more than you are presently? It likely would, but actually it should not. We are on His divine assignment.

Once I was called into the Oval Office of the President of the United States and given an assignment. As I left he did not go with me. My execution of that responsibility was no less diligent than if he had been my companion in performing it. I was under his authority, inspired by his confidence, ennobled by the nature of the task. Being on mission for the president was my motivation. My preoccupation was not with his ability, but his authority. I knew he stood behind what I did because he considered it a worthy task. That made me esteem it all the more worthy of my best. I was at his service even in his absence.

An awareness of our mission being under the authority of Jesus Christ should motivate us to serve Him with all the force, eloquence, dynamism, and even wit He has made available to us. The servant's eye is not on his task but on his master's face. He does not gaze on his toil, but on the Lord of grace. It is not by his commitment he is able to stand, But on that made by the Man of the nail pierced hand. The love of the Master is fervent, That alone motivates a loyal servant.

As the awe struck crowd gazed into the empty sky through which our Lord had ascended, an angel appeared to them. What that heavenly messenger said is easily understood to mean: "Gentlemen, you heard what the Man said, He is coming back. Now, what are you doing hanging around here? Get busy doing what He told you to do".

One does not have to listen too closely to hear heaven and earth reverberate with His charge, "Blessed is that servant, whom his lord when he cometh shall find so doing." Let the service begin!

CHAPTER 8

THE MISTAKES OF A SERVANT

"I have played the fool, and have erred exceedingly." Does that sound like the by-line of your autobiography? Actually it was an expression of Israel's King Saul. It proved to be summary of his life in that it was characterized by foolish mistakes.

Saul's impetuous spirit manifested itself just before he had a major encounter with the Philistine army. It was the ministry of the priest to build an alter and make a sacrifice. Irrepressibly Saul assumed the role of the priest and did it himself. Samuel warned him he had "done foolishly" (I Samuel 13: 13). He had violated the command of the Lord.

Saul's imposing nature showed itself when he "transgressed the commandment of the Lord" by listening to the people and "obeying their voice" (I Samuel 15: 24). Samuel again sternly warned him that this was a foolish mistake.

Saul's imprudent temperament flared in an effort to kill his heir apparent, David. He hunted David like an animal stalking its prey. The futility of the hunt coupled with the grace shown him by David prompted Saul to confess to having played the fool and erred (I Samuel 24: 21).

Saul's implausible character surfaced when he visited the witch of En-dor (I Samuel 28). Any form of the occult has always been abhorrent to the Lord. It was at this point Saul perhaps erred most foolishly. By involving himself in necromancy he showed his lack of dependency upon the Lord whose king he was to be. This mistake sealed his fate. Even those who seek most earnestly to serve make mistakes. "Why?" This is an age old question still in search of an answer. Of even greater importance, what can be done about our mistakes?

Over 2,000 years ago Cicero, the Roman philosopher/statesman, noted what he considered the six mistakes of man:

*   The delusion that personal gain is made by crushing
        others.

*   The tendency to worry about things that cannot be
        changed or corrected.

*   Insisting that a thing is impossible because we cannot
        accomplish it.

*   Refusing to set aside trivial preferences.

*   Neglecting development and refinement of the
        mind, and not acquiring the habit of reading and study.

*   Attempting to compel others to believe and live as we
        do.

Indeed, time hasn't diminished the value of that list. It is a
classic compilation of mistaken concepts. However, there is a
classification of mistakes which might be called "fumbles".

As a young pastor in New Orleans, I once typed our church
bulletin introducing our new minister of music as coming to "Lead us in our
sinning," intending to say "singing".

General Motors had to send out recall notices to 4.9 million
vehicle owners regarding a mistake in the carburetors and exhaust

systems. It was a costly mistake. The postage alone cost more than four million dollars.

The American Marketing Association "Newsletter" contained the following: "It has been brought to our attention that last month we labeled a picture 'Herb Breseman', while the photograph was of Bob Fernald. However, since the article was about Ed Macdonald -- disregard the whole thing."

Alone a highly touted twenty-two year old stood on the vast La Scala Opera stage. This was his big moment to audition for the impresario, Daspuro.

The music started and the young man stood stunned and unresponsive. Belatedly he made a few awkward gestures and equally improper sounds. Then he became silent and dizzy. He had lost control of his mind, voice, and body. In that moment, the young man began to tremble and weep. Off stage a moment later he, the mortified youth, vowed never to sing again. His wise teacher said, "No, no, Little One. We make our climb more slow. And someday -- why, someday La

Scala will come to us." Fortunately for the music world Enrico Caruso overcame his mistake.

Abraham Lincoln's line makes us all feel better: "The man who is incapable of making a mistake is incapable of anything."

A classic case of complex mistakes is recorded in I Samuel 15. Samuel sent Saul on a mission with clear instructions. There was no question as to his assignment. An evaluation of his conduct in light of a few basic principles might help us see ourselves mirrored in such a way as to avoid some of his mistakes.

It can successfully be argued that what Saul did was a sin and not a mistake. Indeed, it was sin. All sin is a mistake though not all mistakes are sins. With that point readily conceded, let's evaluate one of his sins from the vantage point of the mistake involved in committing it.

The Amalekites were foes of Israel from the days of the wilderness. These semi-nomadic people lived on the desert fringe of Southern Palestine. At harvest time, they would raid the fertile regions in search of provisions. Judah's proximity to them made them vulnerable to these attacks.

Samuel was ordered by God to instruct Saul to kill King Agag, all the Amalekites, their sheep, oxen, camels, and donkeys. The command to "utterly destroy" (Verse 3) means they were "devoted to destruction". This extermination is known as a "ban", that is a discipline in which the whole nation participates because of their collective mind-set toward sin. From our perspective that was a ghoulish order. However, when viewed from the vantage point of God and eternity, it is better understood. The Lord desired the land to be occupied by His people as a base from which they could operate without resistance in serving Him. It was with the Amalekites as it is with all people. God doesn't let any person die until that person has reached a permanent mind-set regarding whether to respond positively in receiving Him. Today, that simply means no one dies until he or she has reached a permanent mind-set as to whether or not to receive Christ as Savior. From our earthly vantage point we can't determine this. From His Divine viewpoint He knows when a person has done so.

God knew Agag and all his people had reached a permanent mind-set and nothing could bring them to faith in Him. Again from a supernatural and eternal view point that is the only reason for a person to live.

No human being can tell when another human being has reached a permanent mind-set of rejection. God knew nothing could change their wills. If they had lived for another thousand years, they would not have turned to Him in faith. Therefore, He ordered their annihilation by Saul. This part of the story can only be understood when viewed in light of God's knowledge.

Saul made a major mistake. He killed most of the Amalekites and their animals. However, he decided to spare Agag, a few people, and the best of the animals. This mistake would haunt him until his last breath and actually be responsible for his last breath.

From our retrospective vantage point, we can know what God foresaw and was acting to prevent by turning to the Book of Esther Chapter 3. By doing so we move forward from the time of Saul's disobedience approximately 500 years. In Esther, Haman is described as "the Agagite", that is a descendant of King Agag. "Hamen sought to destroy all the Jews" (Ester 3;6). He wanted "to destroy, to kill, and to annihilate all the Jews, both young and old, little children and women, in one day..." (Ester 3:13). In this way, Hamen, a descendent of those who were to have been destroyed by Saul in order to protect the Messianic line, sought years later to disrupt fulfillment of prophecy regarding Christ's lineage by annihilating all Jews. God's love and knowledge was at work in Saul trying to prevent this.

Character is like glass -- even a little crack shows. What begins as a hair line character flaw in Saul causing his mistake will later shatter his life. Mistakes can be classified in one of three groups with some overlap. Consider these and evaluate which applied to Saul.

CLASSIFICATION OF MISTAKES

DECEPTION. This happens when a person misunderstands a basic aspect of a task. Instructions may not have been clear or the person failed to comprehend them. Deception often results from a person's becoming so absorbed in a minor detail and overlooking the primary purpose. The assignment may be as simple as "button your coat." It is safe to assume the person giving the order desires for the coat to be buttoned in an orderly manner. However, the person buttoning the coat gets so preoccupied with a loose button and frayed buttonhole that he fails to notice he starts by putting button number one in buttonhole number two. As a consequence of this button being wrong, every other button is. This deception isn't detected until the last button is reached. Only then does the deception of the first mistake become obvious. It is essential to be observant and attentive in all things in order to avoid deception as a cause of mistakes.

Saul experienced deception. His was attraction by "all that was good, and were unwilling to utterly destroy them." He carried out orders against what he considered "despised and worthless" (I Samuel 15: 9). Appearance was the deception contributing to his mistake. He forgot what he heard because of what he saw.

DISTRACTION. Often distraction causes a mistake. An attention gaining sight, a sudden unexpected sound, or a physical interference can distract a person just long enough for a major mistake to be make. Such may take only a moment and the consequence be devastating. An exhaustive investigation of a major airline crash killing over 100 people revealed the flight crew was briefly distracted by a flight attendant unexpectedly entering the flight deck shortly after takeoff. In that instance a critical mistake was made ending in tragedy.

Saul became distracted by that which was "best" looking rather that which was best to do. He put his eyes on the flock rather than keeping his mind on his assignment.

DISRUPTION. An act or a thought can disrupt an action or idea. Who hasn't walked into a room, had a momentary disruption, and forgotten what he went into the room for? Who hasn't started to say something, had an instant of disruption and forgotten what he was talking about? Disruptions happen when a more powerful habit or behavior imposes. A strong impulse can cause mental diversion.

This syndrome can be likened to a dog chasing a rabbit. The pursuit is going good when suddenly a deer crosses the trail. The stronger odor of the larger animal catches the attention of the dog and the direction of the chase changes.

Saul had specific instructions, but was disrupted by a stronger impulse. He wanted to keep rather than destroy that which appealed to him.

Servants of the Lord often make mistakes for these reasons. Many fail to follow spiritual orders because of yielding to a strong physical impulse. Many faithful servants have experienced deception, distraction, and/or disruption. As a result many have acted on an earthly impulse rather than a heavenly order. Stories abound about sexual deception, financial distraction, and ambitious disruption. A servant with a mind-set is less likely to consciously make a mistake when causes are identified.

It is imperative for a servant to know his orders clearly and be committed to them completely. Even then minor mistakes will happen.

FIVE MENTAL FUMBLES CAUSING MISTAKES

Samuel met Saul as he returned to Gilgal. Saul made a false report. He said, "Blessed are you of the Lord! I have performed the commandment of the Lord." He made a major mistake and now in trying to cover it he makes another. He lied.

As a youth an old southerner said to me, "One lie is the pappy of another," meaning, if you act out or tell one lie you have to tell another to cover it. Servants should never lie in actions or words.

Saul's report was disrupted by the bleating of sheep and lowing of oxen beyond the mountain ridge where he had hidden them. Samuel asked, "What then is this bleating of sheep in my ears, and the lowing of oxen which I hear?" The sounds of the animals spoke louder than the words of Saul. Facts are stubborn things, and quickly dispatch sophistry. Saul adds the sin of hypocrisy and pretends his action to be religious while in reality it is rebellious. In effect, he says these animals are proof of my devotion to the Lord; they are to be a sacrifice. Selfish overbearing greed is no excuse for disobedience.

What does the revelation of a mistake mean? Our mistakes in judgment or behavior mean something. There is always a reason. There are five basic factors contributing to making mistakes.

INDECISION. The age old question still rings with urgency: "How long halt you between two opinions?" Saul "laid wait in the valley" (Verse 5).

The valley of vacillation has costs many their potential victory. A servant has no reason to vacillate. Slave/servants were trained and experienced at taking orders. They had no cause to hesitate. If a servant heard a command shouted, he had only to determine from whom the command came. If it did not come from his master, it was to be disregarded. If it came from his master, the issue wasn't to obey or not obey, but ownership. Obedience wasn't the issue, ownership was. Obedience was obligatory for a servant. We who profess Christ as Lord don't have a "no" in our vocabulary to use in response to any of His commandments.

Saul sought to excuse his vacillation by saying he "feared the people, and obeyed their voice" (Verse 24). His indecision prepared the seed bed for an improper decision. If he had immediately acted, there would have been no time to listen to the distracting voice of the people. When you have God's opinion, you don't need a second opinion.

Saul was the servant of Samuel in that he was under his command. He acted capriciously and it cost him. He pretended that he fully intended to obey orders. He was going to kill them as ordered, but in stages. He killed most as instructed, but now that he had been caught, he pretended to have brought some back "to sacrifice to the Lord" (Verse 15).

This was obedience by installment. The Lord deserves and demands full payment. Even a worthy sacrifice from a disobedient heart is unacceptable. Delayed obedience is the twin brother of disobedience.

GENERALIZATION. Inadequate planning causes mistakes. Saul started out well. He numbered his troops (verse 4), but he failed to be specific in his instruction.

Nelaton, a renowned French surgeon, said that if he had four minutes to perform an operation on which a life depended, he would take one minute to plan how best to do it.

Saul failed to prescribe what was to be done, how it was to be done, and when it was to be done. Many parents make this mistake in whole or part. They may tell their child to clean up his or her room. The child may comply in part and be scolded only to respond, "You didn't say how good and when." The parent could avoid a mistake by the child by saying, "Clean up your room by putting your blocks in their box, your books on the shelf, and make your bed by 9:00 AM." There would be little doubt about what, how, and when.

Our Master has been very specific with His instructions to His servants. As His servant, inventory what you know He wants you to do that you are not doing. Evaluate how you can do it and establish a time by which you will do it. Don't fail Him because of generalization.

OSSIFICATION. To ossify means to become bone hard. In this instance it is a synonym for being "bull-headed" or if more dignity is desired "stubborn". Such people as these often respond, "Don't confuse me with the facts, I already have my mind made up."

Saul was obstinate, he wanted to conduct the operation his way. Even if he did have the noble intent of wanting belatedly to sacrifice the animals to God, that wasn't what God wanted. For that reason Samuel reminded him "to obey is better than sacrifice" (Verse 22). What the Lord wants is obedience. God knew what was best. It wouldn't be until the end of the story Saul would realize this basic principle.

Failure to listen and learn has crippled many people. Ego plays a big part in the life of an individual who refuses to be open to helpful insights and specific instruction.

Samuel said "stubbornness is as iniquity and idolatry" (Verse 23). Stubbornness makes of one's own self-will an idol to be obeyed rather than the Lord. Only as our will is yielded obediently to the will of our Master can we perform as obedient servants. He must always be the object of our veneration; the one we obey. Conscious disobedience is literally a form of idolatry, because it makes self-will, the human "I", into a god.

A cardinal sin of Christians is failure to be under authority to those God has placed over us. In every organization there has to be a chain of authority. Those under authority who act rebelliously or disrespectfully are resisting God who ordered the structure. All things are to be done decently and in order. When God orders the order honor it. No person should be in authority until they are under authority.

PREOCCUPATION. Saul became preoccupied with "the best" and forgot the right. This contributed to him making his major mistake and failing in his assignment.

When a person gets preoccupied with some minor detail the big picture is lost. Such narrow vision is costly. If a servant of the Lord becomes absorbed in the drudgery of a special detail and loses a sense of mission for the Master, joy and determination is diminished.

Often a preoccupation with a preconceived notion will result in a mistake. Saul evidently had a preconceived misconception of God. His actions indicate he thought God could be compromised. Such a diminished concept of God causes some servants to perform at a level less than their optimum. It produces a blindness.

An excavation near Moundsville, West Virginia, in 1883, opened a chamber containing prehistoric relics. One was a stone tablet inscribed with hieroglyphics which defied translation and were the subject of debate for 92 years.

Approximately 60 linguists studied the characters and in general identified them as Runic, Etruscan or some other ancient language. It wasn't until 1930 that the inscriptions were deciphered. By chance an American glanced at them from a different and odd angle. From his view point he read the message clearly as English spelling out "Bill Stump's Stone, October 14, 1883."

Each of the linguists brought his own preoccupation with him as efforts were made at interpretation. Only objective insight solved the mystery.

A servant's preoccupation should be with the assignment made by his master. Don't miss the big picture of the total task.

AGITATION. A defeating form of agitation is mental fatigue. Short-term memory overload can cause a person to make a mistake. Who hasn't had a time when due to mental overload he simply couldn't think straight. This is a common cause of mistakes.

Even our beloved Lord knew He, in His human form, could not minister out of a bleached-out soul. With the disciples clamoring for Him to respond to a large crowd, He withdrew to rest and pray. Servants of the Lord can have confidence knowing their Master will not assign them more to do than He does time in which to do it.

There is no direct indication this played a part in Saul's mistake. However, neither is there any indication how long the battle that raged "from Havila to Egypt" lasted. It is possible the many military judgment calls he had to make did weary him mentally.

CORRECTING MISTAKES

Servants do make mistakes. Response is more important than the mistake. The mistake is an action. Response is a reaction. Most often we look better in our actions than our reactions. An action is often thought out and a reaction is reflexive. When a mistake is made what should be done?

ACCEPT RESPONSIBILITY. Saul was unwilling to accept responsibility. Even as Samuel was interrogating him the bleating and lowing of the animals beyond the crest of the hill indicated he was lying. Saul was unwilling to accept blame for the mistake in judgment in disobeying orders. Saul greeted Samuel with a lie: "Blessed are you of the Lord: I have performed the commandment of the Lord" (Verse 13).

Character is revealed by what you stand for, fall for, and lie for.

Lies intended to cover failure in fulfilling responsibilities are never right. People respect and admire honest admission, but remain suspicious of those who lie. Chrysler Corporation executives made the mistake of using new cars with mileage indicators disconnected. These vehicles were then sold as new. When this was make public Lee Iacocca, the President of the corporation, went on national news admitting it, apologizing, and announcing a reimbursement program. The mistake, though wrong, was turned into a positive confidence builder for the auto maker.

Saul further refused to take responsibility and persisted in blaming others. He said, "They have brought them...for the people spared the best..." (Verse 15).

Samuel ignored the excuses and went right to the issue of disobedience. It is a sad day in Christendom when a person can almost flippantly say, "I am sorry" and expect to go on as though nothing has happened. An "I am sorry" is no license for self-exoneration.

Obedience is the issue. God prefers things done His way. It is better to obey Him than to do some grandiose deed our way. Samuel put disobedience in perspective when he said of it: "Rebellion is as the sin of witchcraft" (Verse 23). Disobedience and the resulting rebellion is actually defiant self-dependence. It is as evil as witchcraft. Disobedience of the expressed will of God is a malignant sin of so heinous and provocative a nature that it is completely inconsistent with faith in God. It is in effect an act of renunciation of faith. Saul's half converted soul would eventually degenerate into involvement in witchcraft.

When a mistake is made repent of it. Admit it to God as a mistake and turn from it with faith resulting in faithfulness. Don't dwell on the mistake and become remorseful. As with sin, we should come to God confessing and repenting. We should go away, not remorseful over guilt, but rejoicing over grace.

It is the highest form of self-respect to admit making a mistake and to make amends for it. We must be big enough to admit our mistakes, smart enough to profit from them, and strong enough to correct them.

ADVISE OTHERS. Upon realizing a mistake has been made that affects others let them know. Respect will be gained by such openness. Those advised can then take steps to help rectify the mistake. If it is in their interest, others need to know. They likely will recognize the mistake eventually, but if you identify it first, you are respected for your wisdom and honesty.

Saul not only did not advise others, he tried to conceal his major mistake. Samuel had it revealed to him by God. When he knowing it, confronted Saul there was no acknowledgement. Saul first lied, sought to excuse his action, and then blamed others, sought to excuse himself.

When caught he finally reluctantly confessed. The sincerity of his confession is doubtful because even after it he still blamed others. There was no sense of acceptance of his role in the act.

Even if he had delegated the execution as ordered by God, he was still responsible. Delegation is not abdication. Samuel had been the supervisor assigned Saul by God. He knew supervision was a part of delegation. A servant of the Lord in a leadership role must remember he is accountable to God for the good and faithful performance of those he supervises. The servant/supervisor has a multiplied responsibility.

When a mistake is made restitution is appropriate. We should conscientiously seek to amend for our mistakes. Efforts to restore any resulting loss identify sincerity.

ANALYZE IT. An honest evaluation of a mistake can not only help respond properly but prevent it in the future. Saul reviewed his mistake, but he never analyzed it. By diverting attention to the people, he refused to see and admit his role. He persisted in saying, "I have obeyed the voice of the Lord, and have gone on the mission on which the Lord sent me ... But the people took the plunder" (Verses 20,

21). They could not have done it without his approval. Consent would have been a form of conspiracy. This proved to be a character flaw that followed Saul all of his life.

When a mistake is made, learn from it and put it away. Morbidity or moroseness only keeps a person from further productive performance. Forget the incident, but not the lesson learned. Saul never forgot the event and never learned the lesson.

When a mistake is made review it. Evaluate which of the five mental fumbles might have contributed to its occurrence. Consider in which classification it falls: deception, distraction, or disruption.

ASCRIBE A SOLUTION. Saul proposed a solution. Because of a lack of genuine contrition, even his solution was self-centered. Once his error was exposed he in effect said, "Okay, Samuel, I've been caught. Now let's forget the whole thing and let me go on doing things my way." Even when informed that he would not lose his role as physical king, but would rule without supernatural help such as God had offered, he wanted to do it on his own.

The Amalekite King Agag was still alive. According to God's command, which was based on His supernatural insight, he was to have been killed by Saul. Saul made an effort to amend for his mistake by offering to perform the execution. Instead Samuel said to Agag, "As your sword has made women childless, so shall your mother be childless among women. And Samuel hacked Agag to pieces before the Lord in Gilgal" (Verse 33). Samuel had to provide the solution for Saul's failure.

When a mistake is made respond to it in a positive manner. Evasiveness or outright denial is wrong. It only further confuses an already complex situation. A willful positive response reveals character from which productivity can flow.

Saul ruled as king. He did so with the character flaw revealed in these early years manifesting itself in various ways.

Saul's mistake was caused by him wanting to do things his way. God's discipline on him was in permitting him to do things his way all through his life -- even to the end of his life. Samuel warned Saul,

"...you have rejected the word of the Lord, and the Lord has rejected you from being king over Israel" (Verse 26).

One of God's most severe punishments is to let rebellious people have their own way. Thus, the act becomes the punishment. What is seen as good by the rebel is actual protest against God and subject to His discipline. Even Eden without God becomes a jungle.

Daily persons with the mind-set of Saul can be observed. They are people who had great ability, a promising future, and were held in high esteem. Rejecting the will of God and refusing to obey His will, they degenerate into the personification of self-will. They made a mistake and the mistake made them.

Saul, having rejected God, now made it obligatory upon the Lord to reject him. Therefore, "the Spirit of the Lord departed from Saul, and an evil spirit from the Lord troubled him" (I Samuel 16: 14). All through Saul's life ran the maddening elements of discord. Day after day the higher and lower fought within him for the throne of his divided heart. Daily he awakened to hear two voices vying for his loyalty. His heart was never right with God and consequently never at peace. Even when he chose the good he looked wistfully on the lower. When he chose the worse he trembled at the very thought of God.

Saul's rejection of God was made evident by his false pious proclamation of devotion when he said, "the people spared the best of the sheep and of the oxen, to sacrifice to the Lord your God" (Verse 15). Notice he said "your God" not "my God".

God did not reject Saul because of a single act of inconsequential disobedience. He knew his heart to be in an abiding stated of rebellion that would never change. Just as the Lord knew the hardened, never to repent hearts of the Amalekites, so He knew the permanent mind-set of Saul. He knew what Saul had set himself to be once and for all.

In the New Testament those who indulge in obstinate self-will are described as being "given over" by God. That is, He lets them have their own will without His will. That becomes the punishment of the disobedient.

As Samuel concluded his reprimand Saul lunged at him tearing his robe in the desperate act. Samuel warned "The Lord has torn the kingdom of Israel from you" (Verse 28). Saul reigned as king in his own way, but without the blessing of the Spirit of the Lord being on him. His was forever to be a divided kingdom as symbolized by the torn robe. Years lapsed. The rule of Saul floundered. He never properly responded to the Lord. His first mistake resulted in his last.

Time lapsed and Saul, the seasoned warrior, lay wounded on the battlefield. Suddenly there appeared standing over him the form of a young man. As the youth raised Saul's own sword to deliver the death blow Saul asked, "Who are you?" The answer, "I am an Amalekite."

Saul's mistake had come full circle. One who survived because of his disobedience became the agent of his destruction.

Everybody makes mistakes. It is imperative that we deal with them before they deal with us. Years ago W.T. Purkiser gave this anatomy of Saul's mistake:

> Partial obedience (Verses 3 & 9)
>
> Professed faithfulness (Verses 12, 13)
>
> Public failure (Verses 14 - 19)
>
> Poor excuse (Verses 20, 21)

Prophetic rebuke (Verses 22, 23)

Pretended repentance (Verses 24 - 27)

Predicted destruction (Verses 28 - 31).

This tragic sequence of degeneration and deterioration can be avoided if the following steps are taken.

* Repent of any mistake. That doesn't mean to merely be sorry or even grieve over it. It means to agree with God's opinion of it and turn from it. Avoid mentally loitering around a mistake. Make sure it is an isolated event not an ongoing process. Self-flagellation does no good. Name it to God as being what it was and rejoice over loving acceptance.

* Restitution is appropriate in some cases. If someone sustains a loss physically or emotionally, seek to restore what can be restored. This not only builds the confidence of others it is a superb stimulus to future self-discipline. When mistakes become as costly to us as to others we seek even harder to avoid them.

*   Review your mistake. Realize all conscientious servants make mistakes. Don't let the fact you make one keep you from further productive efforts. If having made one, retards future efforts it is not only a mistake it is a defeat. By reviewing a mistake, insight can be gained as to how to avoid similar ones in the future. Never let a mistake keep you from your best effort in future acts of service.

*   Respond to your mistakes as a student having learned a vital lesson. Let it be a motivating factor driving you to more faithful service. To become morbid or morose, is to make a second mistake related to the same issue. Resolve to be attentive to deception, distraction, an disruption in the future in order to avoid mistakes.

The biggest mistake young Caruso could have made would have been to keep his emotional vow never to sing again. A servant who resigns from the "service core" because of a mistake has made two mistakes.

Caruso overcame his major mistake. La Scala did come to him and along with it Europe, South America, Russia, England, and America. His clarion voice made his entire life a pageant of triumph. He sang his way into the hearts of millions melting barriers of race, nationality, and language. Through song he enabled people to realize their oneness. History records few names of persons who quit because of mistakes.

Those recorded are most often noted as quitters. Annals are replete with the names of those who recovered from mistakes and lived to serve as never before. Those who resolve to let their mistakes make them better servants not only make fewer mistakes -- they make better servants. A servant's mind must be on his Master not his mistake.

THE MONITOR OF A SERVANT

Are you willing to start monitoring yourself to see if you have a true servant temperament?

The following test may reveal for you admirable traits which you presently have. It may also challenge you to develop in some areas you have overlooked. Grade yourself on it now. Evaluate the areas of strength and weakness. Make a mental note of areas where improvement is needed. Take the test again in one month and see how you have progressed.

Be truthful. Be objective. Don't be overly critical of yourself. Neither should you pamper yourself in arriving at an honest appraisal of yourself as a servant.

AS A SERVANT DO YOU ...?

	YES	NO
GIVE OF YOURSELF "Jesus emptied himself"		
HUMBLE YOURSELF (under the mighty hand of God)		
CONSIDER THE NEEDS OF OTHERS BEFORE YOUR OWN		
OBEY DIVINE AND HUMAN AUTHORITY		

HAVE A SENSE OF MISSION; IS YOUR PURPOSE SERVICE

HAVE INTEGRITY IN ALL THINGS

SHOW DETERMINATION TO SERVE (STICK-TO-IT-NESS)

SUBMIT YOURSELF TO ALL RESPONSIBLE REGULATIONS

SHOW SENSITIVITY TO THE NEEDS OF OTHERS

FAITHFULLY FULFILL LITTLE NEEDS

EVIDENCE DEPENDABILITY

ACCOMPLISH ASSIGNMENTS IN A TIMELY MANNER

WILLINGLY ASSUME APPROPRIATE RESPONSIBILITY

LIVE WITHIN LEGITIMATE STRUCTURE

SEEK THE GOOD OF THE GROUP INVOLVED

SACRIFICE FOR THE COMMON GOOD

GO THE "EXTRA MILE" (DO MORE THAN REQUIRED)

WORK AS A "HOLE PLUGGER"(FILL THE LITTLE ROLES)

SHOW RESPECT FOR OTHERS BY ALWAYS BEING ON TIME

HOW CAN YOU TELL A SERVANT?

BY THE SERVICE PERFORMED.

"BY THEIR FRUIT YOU SHALL KNOW THEM".

QUOTES FROM

SERVANTS NOT CELEBRITIES
By: Nelson L. Price

Chapter 1 - "The Meaning of Servanthood"

"Self-esteem, happiness as an end in itself, recognition, notoriety, self- assertiveness, and prosperity theology are themes that sell today. Motivated by such themes we have turned inward rather than turning loose and, as a result, we have become stagnant rather than flowing with life. Having been created to give of ourselves, we have instead become emotional statuary waiting for a proper pedestal. "How may I gain and attain" has replaced "how may I serve you in the name of my Lord."

"A servant temperament more than any other trait makes for a productive person. This trait takes precedent over education, personality, and skill. It determines how effectively one will use all other admirable assets. It identifies one as having compassion, being conscientious, and showing concern. Skills can be taught but this basic characteristic must come from the core of the individual's will. A gifted person without a servant temperament cannot contribute as much to society as a less talented person with a servant temperament."

"There are many modern examples of persons deeply involved in 'selling' Christianity who have fallen away. For a period of time they gave every external evidence of being a believer. Their achievements have in some instances earned them the status of a celebrity. Their external charade, inevitably, is exposed and their apostate nature revealed. These are decoys of Satan and alibies of sinners. We must not be deceived by such persons for hypocrisy is the tribute vice pays to virtue."

Chapter 2 - "The Mindset of a Servant"

"The faith that works is a faith that works." "Why call Christ Master and not follow Him?"
"Why call Him King of Kings and not serve Him?" "Why call Him Lord of Lords and not obey Him? "Why?"

"Part of servanthood consists in learning how the master wants things done, how he does them, and doing them his way."

"For a servant/disciple the Bible becomes the procedures manual. If we accept what we like in the Bible and reject what we dislike, it is not the Bible we believe but ourselves."

"A true servant/disciple looks up to his master. You may have been looking back in disappointment. You may have been looking forward in despair. You may have been looking within in despondency. These habits can only be broken by looking up in delight."

Chapter 4 - "The Motivation of a Servant"

Christ meets us at the crossroads of life and shows us which way to go by walking with us. That fellowship sustains even if the pilgrimage goes through the valley of the shadow of death. It is the companion, not the country, that makes the journey. The nature of things around us may tend to make us disloyal. Fellowship with Christ makes us loyal servants."

"No person is truly free if undisciplined. Great discipline is needed by a musician in order to best be able to improvise. Discipline is required for an athlete to innovate. Greater discipline is required by a servant to be able to render spontaneous service. The more nearly perfect the discipline the more joyous the service."

Chapter 5 - "The Model of a Servant"

"Never judge a journey by its route alone. Follow the trail until you find where it ends. A fact can be learned one of two ways: experientially or academically. If we academically learn the ends of the routes of being "servants of uncleanness" and being "servants to righteousness unto holiness" we can spare ourselves much experiential misery."

"I am convinced that the only proper spirit of a true servant of the Lord is that "He must increase and I must decrease."

Chapter 6 - "The Mentality of a Servant"

"A servant is a servant regardless of the circumstances."

"To Christ obedience was always the true test of love. He never hinted that love was simple sentiment or erratic emotion. It is the thread in the fabric of life that never fades no matter how often it is washed in the water of grief and adversity."

"Faithful service is the insignia of a loving heart."

"A miracle, after all, is only a miracle from our perspective. For God it is all in a day's work."

"Someday our molded, physical remains will be all that evidences our former presence on this planet. Then faithful obedient service to the words of our Lord will have just begun to pay dividends in Heaven."

"The traditions of man are fallacious and fallible. The text of God's Word is tried and true. Nevertheless, our opinion of it is not as important as our obedience to it."

"Those who serve Christ can only do so consistently if they have a mind- set and interpret the things that happen to them as opportunities to serve."

"The Law of Emotional Gravity dominates a life without an orientation of Biblical obedience. Simply stated, it is: "one pessimist can pull five optimists down easier than five optimists can lift up one pessimist."

"The servant's eye is not on his task but on his master's face." "He does not gaze on his toil but on the Lord of grace."
"It is not by his commitment he is able to stand,"
"But on that made by the Man of the nail pierced hand." "The love of the Master is fervent,"
"That alone motivates a loyal servant."

Nelson L. Price

Quotes from the manuscript thesis:

"Jesus 'rose from supper and laid aside His garments, took a towel and girded Himself. After that, He poured water into a basin and began to wash the disciples' feet, and to wipe them with the towel with which He was girded" (John 13:4, 5).

"Jesus 'made Himself of no reputation, taking the form of a servant..." (Philippians 2:7).

"It is enough for a servant that he be as his master. Therefore, take up your towel and follow Christ."

"This is an invitation to join the Royal Order of the Towel."

Servants Not Celebrities

Nelson Price

Copyright Nelson Price 2014

Published by Nelson Price Ministries, Inc.

Visit the web site of Nelson Price for over 200 articles on
Bible topics and current events:
www.nelsonprice.com

Made in the USA
Middletown, DE
19 August 2023

36982608R00139